ANDRÉ VEENSTRA

Handbook of Ship Modelling

Model & Allied Publications,
Argus Books Limited

Model & Allied Publications
Argus Books Ltd
Argus House
14 St James Road
Watford
Herts
England

First published 1981

ISBN 085242 714 X

© Kluwer Technische Boeken BV – Deventer – Antwerp
English translation © Argus Books Ltd. 1981

Typeset by Inforum Ltd, Portsmouth
Printed and Bound by A. Wheaton & Co., Ltd., Exeter

Contents

1

Foreword

The object of this book is to give you the most important practical data and insight into the building of boat and ship models in general, and of models without radio control in particular. There are no extensive descriptions of modelling 16th and 17th century ships, sometimes known as period ships, since the building of these and the problems associated with them need a book to themselves.

The content of this book is based entirely on practice. In addition to descriptions of a number of simple mechanical and electronic systems, it also discusses the best choice of material for the various model categories. The use of all types of tools is not forgotten, and there are sections on the use of various sorts of adhesives, soldering and other methods of jointing, control and propulsion motors, propellers, couplings, sails and sailing, charging of batteries, etc.

This book will be of assistance to the beginner who, taking a piece of wood, a hammer, a saw, a pair of pliers and a tube of glue, and perhaps a propulsion unit, wants to build a model boat or ship. It attempts to answer the questions "How do I go about it, where do I start, and what must I watch out for?". It is a guide to setting up the "home shipyard", and it will lead to the acquisition of an absorbing and useful hobby. It goes even further, in giving some ideas and descriptions of experimental prototypes, some of which have already been proven in practice. However, in many cases, it is still up to the reader to adapt and improve them in his own way.

Some examples of the sort of thing included are bow thrusters, fire pumps, and automatic coupling and uncoupling of tow ropes.

The book does not discuss construction of home-built radio control equipment, but does provide a basic guide to what is generally available commercially and discusses basic installation techniques, and where necessary, indicates the appropriate book to refer to. Although this book is primarily intended for the beginner, the more experienced modeller should find several useful aspects to it, and be able to use it to refresh his memory. At the back of the book, there are tables of the most commonly used electric motors and their characteristics, as well as a list of useful radio-control systems, wiring, etc.

5

I hope that, with the help of this book, you will not only set a good ship to water, but also be able to get the most out of your ship modelling.

Andre Veenstra

1 Model ship building in general

The history of model ship building is really just as old as seafaring itself. A visit to various museums shows that model ship builders existed as long ago as the Phoenicians and the Egyptians. They made charming models of their primitive craft from clay and wax. Many of these have been found as relics in pyramids and royal tombs. Three excellent examples were found in the burial chamber of Tutankhamen. These are executed very beautifully and in great detail. Probably even more interesting are those that were found in the tomb of another Pharaoh, Mekt-Re. Here a fishing boat was found together with a pleasure craft that had a cabin containing a bed. There was also a larger boat of the same type plus an escort boat for the royal court that was fitted out with a kitchen that included a stove. These models were made for religious purposes and were intended to serve the Pharaoh after his death.

1.1. Antique Burmese model ship.

Centuries later, around the fifteenth century, the famous Spanish Mataro model, also executed in great detail, was built. The growth of seafaring in the 16th and 17th centuries with daring voyages to the Far East and to the coasts of North and South America was accompanied by just as sharp an increase in the building of model ships as in the building of real ships. These models were completely hand-carved. As far as is known the most beautiful models of this period were made in England.

The idea of building models with a view to mimicking the behaviour of real ships originated mainly with a certain Phineas Pett – an English ship builder. He made a model of the Ark Royal for Prince Henry, the eldest son of James the First. Later he made two more models, the Prince Royal and the Sovereign of the Seas.

Models for study

Oliver Cromwell ordered that a model of every ship design should be delivered to the then Lords Commissioners, probably because the Lords found it too difficult to imagine the details of a ship, simply from the construction drawings. Partly for this reason models of the time were often made with a hull that was wholly or partly unplanked, so that the form of the ribs, etc., could be clearly seen. Later models were planked to the water line. This is contrary to what was done elsewhere in Europe at that time where it was customary to plank the model completely.

Regrettably, many models were destroyed by military action in World War Two. Fortunately, plenty remain and can be admired in such museums as the National Maritime Museum at Greenwich, the Science Museum and the Imperial War Museum in London, as well as in other museums in Europe, examples being Rotterdam, Amsterdam and Antwerp. Among others to be seen at Greenwich are model ships made during the Napoleonic wars by French prisoners of war. It is amazing how faithful and detailed these models are considering how little information the prisoners had at their disposal. Many are of bone, but materials used include bed straw and scraps of wood including box wood.

8

Early in the 19th century a start was made in America with the use of models for test purposes. Only a few of these remain, partly through trade secrecy and partly due to the decline in the American ship-building industry that took place after the Civil War.

With the coming of the steam engine and the changeover from wooden hulls to steel, many shipping companies began

1.2.   The famous American 'Constitution' is a very popular period model.

to use models for commercial purposes and in their advertising, in order to attract passengers (and crew). Quietly, various navies began to copy the example of the civil lines. And not only to attract recruits: the models were also used for training purposes. It was easier to illustrate naval terminology, to teach ship recognition and to show the construction and parts of a ship. The models were also used to demonstrate sea battles and tactical manoeuvres. Since the beginning of the present century model ships have often been built for professional purposes. The most important form is the construction of models for the test tanks of the maritime research institutes.

In test tanks (towing tanks) of research establishments such as that at Greenwich, accurately scaled hulls are towed through the water by carriages that straddle the tanks. Instruments mounted on the hull and the carriage collect data relating to the water resistance of the hull, its stability and manoeuvrability.

Model ships for recreation

Recreational model ships have in large measure become popular thanks to the toy and hobby industry. The admiration and pride that members of seafaring nations have for the merchant and naval fleets is evidenced by models, often self-made, which in Victorian times formed a standard part of the house furnishings. Even building ships in bottles, although of Far Eastern origin, became a domestic hobby.

The sight of a youngster sailing his toy boat in the local pond was one of the things that inspired adults to build models for sailing. The hobby industry was ready and eager to supply construction materials, kits, and the requisite parts. There is currently a wide variety of models on offer, for sailing as well as for decoration. England, Germany, the Scandinavian countries, Japan and America are the foremost suppliers. This is also true for radio control equipment.

The would-be model builder has a wide choice both in material and methods: wood, plastic, metal or paper; from a complete kit or from a blueprint. If he has no interest in sailing he can choose a decorative model or a waterline model. The latter are model ships built from the waterline up; they are, thus, flat-bottomed without keel, rudder or screw. He who chooses to make a model for sailing has not only the pleasure of construction in the winter months but also that of sailing his model in the spring and summer.

Furthermore, a model ship that really sails gives a much more realistic impression. With the help of modern radio control equipment a very high degree of realism can be attained, and much of the model's equipment can be operated just as in the original ship. Anchors can be dropped and weighed, derricks can turn, water cannon can extinguish a fire, cables for towing or rescue can be fired to another ship, in warships the guns can be laid and fired, radar and/or fire control equipment can rotate, searchlights can be switched on and off. And all from the bank.

One can sail one's model alone or join a club for constructors and sailers. This has the advantage of assistance with problems, the participation in contests and demonstrations. This subject is treated at greater length elsewhere in this book. By being able to trade experiences with fellow hobbyists and by

1.3.   Beautifully detailed model of the heavy cruiser Admiral Hipper (Imperial War Museum, London).

the discovery and development of new ideas the art of model ship building becomes more and more refined.

Modern electronics and refined tools, by reason of their accuracy and usefulness, offer so much extra pleasure in both construction and sailing and inspire to the realisation of so many ideas that a model ship builder is able to construct a model of virtually any real or imaginary ship. At the same time, the development of ingenuity and the will-power needed to create something, the study of such a variety of background material and subjects such as mechanical engineering and electronics have considerable educational value.

1.4.   Example of scale model kits that can be bought (Adolph Bermpohl by Graupner).

Model ship building has also social aspects because apart from the enjoyment derived by the model builder (and his family), others can also take pleasure in his hobby. Competitions and demonstrations are attended by droves of people – an attendance of two or three thousand is not unusual. The consequence is that the model builder is motivated to make the best possible showing and approaches his hobby with even more ardour, an ardour which is fanned by the breadth of choice available, something to suit everyone's pocket. It can be as expensive or as inexpensive as one wishes.

Naturally a ship that only sails and steers and is no longer than 60 cm, for example, is much cheaper to acquire than a ship of 2 metres in which everything works, down to the last detail. But isn't it the same with everything? Accessories and material have a considerable effect on price. If one intends building a decorative model (that either doesn't or can't sail), radio control equipment is unnecessary. If one does intend to sail the model then one should acquire good radio control equipment at the outset, and equipment that lends itself to later extension.

It often happens that, because of the cost, one begins with a cheap transmitter, receiver and servos, for example equipment with only two channels, that is, with two functions (we will go into this later). One function is then for controlling the power source and one for the steering mechanism. However, the more experience one gains the greater the will and the capacity to do more. One can't add a working crane or a pump because all the channels are occupied. So one considers the acquisition of control equipment having more functions, which will either have to be bought or constructed. The old equipment is consigned to the cupboard which is a waste of the money one invested in it. Better, then, to save a little longer, wait a couple of months, and acquire at the outset good equipment that allows for later extension. It is not essential that one acquires everthing at once, as long as the opportunity for extension is there. The money is well invested and you don't have unused and unusable equipment left lying around.

Starting is always difficult

When one goes to the model shop, enthusiastic but inexperienced, and with a well-filled wallet, it is as well to realise that there are many kits that, while extremely attractive and alluring are extremely difficult for a novice. One gets by, but don't ask how!

Often the construction drawing in the kit is misread and mis-interpreted. Some insight is needed in reading a drawing because it is a two-dimensional picture of a three-dimensional object – a ship on a flat surface. Furthermore, some drawings contain, regrettably, errors, as a result of which some parts turn out later either not to fit, or to fit badly.

Some attention should also be paid to the material of the kit. Is it fully prepared by the manufacturer or not? If so, one can see the pre-cut and prepared parts in the packet. Are all the small, but essential, parts included? By these we mean portholes, lifeboats, anchors, capstans, masts, tackle and rigging, rail-ings, flagstaffs, lamps, searchlights, etc. (see in the fore-ground of Fig. 1.5).

They are sometimes included and sometimes not. If not, then one must either make or buy, and a complete set of parts can add up to quite a bit of money.

In some kits the hull is either wholly or partly prepared, and there are also ready-to-use plastic hulls available. In some imported kits, an English (more or less) translation of the

1.5.   There is choice enough in the model shop (Gerrése, Model dept., The Hague).

instructions is included. Where not, or where the translation is poor, one has to fall back on one's personal ingenuity and ability to read the drawings.

There are plenty of well-known brands available, such as Graupner, Billing Boats, Simprop, Aeronaut and Svensson. Some of these manufacturers also supply their own range of control systems.

Don't choose too difficult a model to start with. Just where the border-line is, is difficult to say but a small pleasure boat can be recommended. Judge for yourself and don't be afraid to say that you are a novice. A good model shop will always be ready to give sound advice.

Although a ready-made hull may sound attractive it won't help you learn model boat-building. If you just want to try your hand at boat-building then such a ready-made hull is all right, but if you are thinking of boat-building as a hobby it is best to master the art of hull construction as early as possible.

Above all, don't be misled by such terms as 'built in a jiffy', they give the impression that a single evening is sufficient for

1.6.   Don't start too ambitiously, a model like this is difficult enough to begin with (de Lang, NL).

making the model and that you will be sailing with it the following week-end. It is simply a sales stunt of the manufacturer! Certainly some of the sawing and cutting has been done and that does save time, but the hobby is much more interesting when one does as much as one can oneself. In any case such kits are more expensive than others; after all, more work has been put into them.

Furthermore, in the kit the design is fixed. There is little chance that one can modify or adapt the design should that prove necessary. For example, one may want to build-in a larger battery or motor, to have the decks fixed or removable. Modifying a construction drawing is no simple task, especially if the changes affect fundamental parts of the ship, bearing in mind that one mustn't weaken the structure or alter the scale.

Among the well-known plastic kits for model ships there are a number that can be radio controlled, but most of them are either too small or otherwise unsuitable. If one wants to make one of the few that are capable of sailing, one can, of course. The advantage is that all the parts are ready-made and only need cementing together.

Nonetheless, many problems can arise during construction and it doesn't do to take such kits lightly. In a few cases such a kit contains as many as 600 parts from which a beautiful ship can be built. Painting, too, must be well done. A well built ship

1.7.   The Yamato by Nichimo is a plastic kit comprising some 600 parts (the author).

badly finished with ugly paintwork gives no satisfaction. In short, be critical in acquiring your first model, consult the catalogues of the various manufacturers, and consider which radio control equipment you will buy and instal. Is there enough room for it? A too difficult model to begin with brings only misery in place of pleasure and relaxation. One leaves it half finished unless one gets help. Begin simply, therefore.

Why model ships?

Most Europeans, the Dutch and the British in particular, think highly of model ship building. Why is this? There are reasons. In the first place the Dutch have always been a people who have to defend themselves against water, but have also been, for centuries, one of the greatest seafaring nations in the world. It is more or less a national characteristic, this interest in seafaring and the attraction of water. It is just the same with the British.

In brief, if anyone sees a model ship then his heart begins to beat faster and simultaneously with the enthusiasm the thought arises 'Could I make something like that?'. Usually it stops at the thought, but many go to work and after some time proudly exhibit their first model, whatever it looks like.

A second aspect of model ship building is that in most countries, and certainly in ours, there is always room for sailing.

If one wishes simply to build decorative models then the problems of movement do not arise and neither do the problems of water on which to sail.

2   Model types and scales

There are, of course, a great number of vessels that are at one moment called ships and at another boats. Actually it is a distinction without precise definition. Larger vessels can be classified as ships: passenger ships, freighters, warships, for example, and smaller vessels as boats, sail boats, motor boats, rowing boats, steam boats, tugs, etc. The last named are generally smaller. But even this difference is not always valid, and the two terms can be used pretty well interchangeably. We will do that in this book.

Just as in shipping in general, the number of types of models

2.1.   The advanced model builder seeks something exclusive such as this tugboat, the Moorcock (K.A. Gramende, NL).

is pretty well unlimited. However, not all sorts of ship are available as kits nor can one always obtain a construction drawing from the model shop. Usually kit manufacturers or importers offer what the public demands and, furthermore, take account of the skills and technical knowledge of the average purchaser, which means that the degree of difficulty is adapted to Mr. Average.

One should also remember that the more complicated the kit, the more accessories there are, and the more internal and external adaptations to simplify construction, the higher the price. The manufacturer can permit himself but a few complex kits in his range because they are rarely bought by beginners, and it is the beginner rather than the expert who usually buys kits. The expert seeks rather something exclusive and is more likely to work from a construction drawing or even from a shipyard blueprint. The last named can be acquired from a shipyard, at least, provided the ship is not of recent date. This is because of the dangers of competition and industrial espionage, and is doubly true when the subject is a warship.

The Office of Maritime History in The Hague possesses countless drawings of Dutch Naval ships and one can, with luck, sometimes obtain a drawing from them, provided it is solely and exclusively used for model building. Only in the event that the subject is an out-of-date ship can one be certain of obtaining a drawing. For modern warships one must content oneself with the illustrations in magazines and books. Actually this is true of all modern ships. One can write direct to a shipbuilder, one can also try The Netherlands Navigation Union in The Hague or the United Netherlands Shipyards, also in The Hague. Another good place is the Central Maritime Foundation in Harlem who can assist the interested model builder with addresses or can make their own literature list available. Construction from a (shipyard) blueprint is really only for the advanced model builder.

In the United Kingdom, apart from the commercial plan suppliers, the National Maritime Museum, Greenwich, London, SE10 and Ministry of Defence (Navy), Section 423B, Foxhill, Bath, Avon, can often assist with warship plans and photographs.

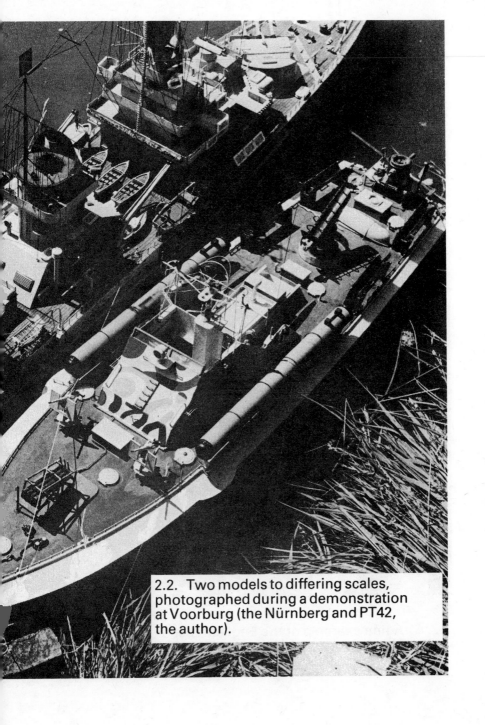

2.2. Two models to differing scales, photographed during a demonstration at Voorburg (the Nürnberg and PT42, the author).

Modification

Back to the manufacturer's standard kit. One sees that a number of models are available, in rising degree of difficulty. Compared with the past there are now more complex kits available. Manufacturers who keep their eye on the market have observed that the technical know-how of the hobbyist has reached the point that such terms 'provision for working water hydrants', 'working towing bollards', 'lifeboats can be lowered', are accepted as everyday.

Most of these developments stem from the demonstrations and contests organised by clubs. Model builders are usually proud of their own developments and are prepared to let everyone see them. The manufacturer is therefore in a position to learn what can be done with various parts and can assess the public interest and adapt his product thereto.

2.2.   A fine example of the English Vosper MTB. A plastic kit model served as example (A. Bedet, NL).

Apart from the fact that it is often difficult for the model constructor to achieve a realistic working of some functions, the control aspects also become more complex. One needs a transmitter with more functions, which means that the cost of the control equipment rises, and, of course, the cost of the kit is higher. Manufacturers not only keep an eye on the spare time that their public have, they also keep an eye on the amount of money they are prepared to spend. Today, many are ready, willing and able to afford £50 or more for hobby expenditure. One can keep prices down by, for example, buying a fairly simple model and building one's own accessories. As a hobby, model ship building is not particularly cheap, but one can find a happy medium.

By making some parts for oneself one also exercises ones ingenuity, and there is always much more satisfaction in designing and building oneself than in buying ready-made. Of course when something comes with the kit one can do little else but use it.

Limited choice

However broad the range of kits displayed in the shops may seem, the number of radio controlled models from each

2.3. The tugboat Oceanic is a very popular model.

manufacturer is actually pretty limited. What is on display in the shop is a collection derived from the ranges of various manufacturers. If one buys something from the selection one can be pretty certain that someone else has the same model. Nothing unique, therefore. What have the manufacturers to offer who stock up the shopkeeper? In most catalogues one will find: one or two tugboats, a few leisure motor craft, a fishing vessel, a fire tender, a warship, a freighter, a police launch or patrol boat and a few sailing boats.

Some brands have a specific series in their range, like Aeronaut, with their range of warships, including a battleship, a cruiser and a submarine, all to the same scale (see elsewhere in this book). Billing Boats, on the other hand, don't have a single warship in their range, but they do have a splendid Swedish ferry boat from 1910. Most kits contain parts of wood and plastic and a drawing or a diagram from which the model can be built. All these models are suited to building in radio control apparatus. Their lengths run from 60 cm to about 135 cm.

For the beginner there are plenty of kits to choose from. Apart from wooden models there are also plastic ones which, with a little care, can be adapted to radio control. The Japanese manufacturer 'Nichino' has a range of warships of which the battleship 'Yamato' is most suitable for radio control. This (large) kit for a ship of 138 cm length contains some 600 ready-to-use parts which can be fitted together with plastic cement or plastic solvent. An instruction sheet (in Japanese and English) with various illustrations leads the model builder through construction.

Anyone who thinks that this sort of model is easier to make than a wooden one has got it completely wrong. It is often really more difficult because careless workmanship (e.g. using a little too much cement or solvent with the smaller parts) leads irrevocably to an ugly model. This is just as true of painting and finishing. Making an accessory oneself from wood (or even plastic) not only gives ugly results, it is often not even possible because of the smallness of the parts. A further disadvantage for plastic kits is the problem of making them water tight. Rubber strips and other means can help, but we will deal with that later.

One must not, of course forget the decorative models. These

are the ones that are built purely for their decorative value or as part of a collection, complete series being available.

There are countless kits of this sort under such various brands as Revell, Tamiya, Nichimo, Airfix, Aurora, to mention but a few. Some advanced model builders buy such a decorative model and use it as an example for building a sailing model of the same ship (see Fig. 2.2).

Prepared or unprepared material

Among the decorative ship models must be counted the 'period' models such as, galleons, barques, clippers, schooners, brigs, etc., that really form a chapter apart, especially seeing the difficulties that the construction, the tackle and the rigging can give. Furthermore, the construction of such ships differs from the construction of those that usually fall under sailing models. These old servants (beautiful as they are) are not to be recommended to beginners. The firm of Steingraeber is specialised in this type of model, and the Aeropiccola brand has very fine kits of old and very old ships.

Simprop has also included one in their range. In the catalogue they make a fine showing. These, generally speaking, well-made kits, complete with accessories are more than worth the trouble of building, even if the prices are a bit of an eye-opener. Some models can be adapted to sail, albeit with some sacrifice to the model. For example, the lowest line of cannon ports have to be cemented closed to keep out the water. A good deal of ballast (lead) must be used and all masts, sails, jibs, gaffs and yards as well as all the rigging, need to be adapted. This is no easy task, especially if one has no insight into or knowledge of the construction of the ship in question. Furthermore, such a square rigged ship can scarcely ever be sailed close to the wind.

With all these kits it is the intention that the material supplied is finished off oneself by sawing, cutting, sanding, planing and cementing. The last may or may not be combined with nailing or screwing. In some kits a part of the material is pre-prepared by the manufacturer, with numbered and scored or sawn parts, or with ready-to-use parts. The numbering of the parts relates to the numbers used in the construction drawing. A few kits even contain a ready built hull which

2.4.   Plastic kits are more difficult than they seem. The detail here is excellent. (Yamato)

reduces construction time immensely. In the hull one must install such parts as the motor(s), radio control equipment, energy source(s), propeller shaft(s), etc. By the way, a good model maker chooses the propulsion of the ship first and then builds the ship around it. Elsewhere in this book we will show how true this statement is. For the beginner such a ready-to-use hull offers the advantage that the most difficult work has been done for him.

The rest of the construction is usually also fairly well prepared: deckhouses, decks, funnels, lifeboats, etc., are all either roughly finished or ready-to-use. In some cases one only needs to finish the parts off, mount them, sand off and paint. In theory, at least; in practice it often turns out otherwise. The kits do not normally include screws, motor(s), radio control, power source(s) and cement. Sometimes propeller shafts and propellers are included and, very rarely, the accessories; it depends on the brand.

Scale

The kits that we have until now considered are the scale models; models that within a certain scale are faithful copies

2.5.   A police boat that has been adapted to Coast Guard vessel; made from deep drawn plastic and pre-sawn wooden parts (the author).

of the real ships. There are various standard scales, standardisation being necessary both for the manufacturers of the parts and of the kits, as well as for the model builder. Common among sailing models are: 1 to 25 (written 1:25), 1:50, 1:75, 1:100, and 1:200. In the decorative models it goes even further, up to 1:1200. Should one, when designing and building oneself, come out between the standard scales, then one must choose the nearest standard scale for the parts. In practice this is less of a problem than one might think; the eye can scarcely detect the difference. In the course of this book it will become clear that scale relationships are the basis on which the total construction of the model together with its propulsion system (assuming it is motor driven) depends. In fact the same is true for sailing ships, but to a lesser extent.

The scale of kits and model ships is to some extent determined by the ranges of parts and accessories that are available. This is logical, of course; if one tried to use an anchor to a scale of 1:25 with a model to a scale of 1:100 it would turn out too large. Reverse the scale relationship and the anchor would be too small.

It is true that many manufacturers can supply a full range of

Fig. 2.6. Stern of the tugboat Aegir. Note the detail, for example the fire extinguisher. The scale is 25/1.
(H.K.J. v.d. Bussche, NL).

general accessories for all the standard scales, but if one wants something special then one must bear in mind the scale of the ship. This is of very great importance in choosing the propeller shaft, propeller(s) and electric motor(s). This will be extensively dealt with in the chapter on propulsion and steering.

With scale models, as distinct from model racing boats, one sails gently. The speed should be the 'scale' speed. By means of an electronic control one is able continuously to vary the speed via a receiver on the ship that responds to a transmitter in one's hand. One can either increase or reduce speed depending on whether one advances or retards the stick on the transmitter in one's hand. The same principle is used for steering which is also continuously variable; one can continue ahead or one can gently steer to port or starboard.

This continuously variable control is only applicable if one uses a proportional or digital transmission system with appropriate servos. There are now outdated systems, the so-named pulse systems, which require a certain dexterity for good results. However, proportional control is the one most used today, and offers the advantages of simpler operation and more direct control. A more practical description of the application of this equipment will be found elsewhere in this book.

Scale models have the advantage that apart from sailing and

steering, actual working functions can be built-in. That this tests the ingenuity of the builder and gives free play to his imagination need not be stressed. The choice of scale model is, in the first place, dependent on the taste of the constructor; a second consideration is the degree of difficulty in building; the third (and often the most important) is the amount of cash available. It is fine to imagine all the different functions one can assign to one's model, provided, of course, that they are applicable to the model in question; it is another thing to do it. However, novice model constructors have the tendency to think up ideas that will make their model that little bit more real than their neighbour's (who has been at it for years).

3 Space, tools, materials

Before that first bold step to a model shop with a view to acquiring a kit for an attractive model, it is as well first to take a look, certainly as regards the size of the model, at the amount of space one has available at home, or wherever one intends building. One needs, in fact, a fair amount of space to build a model, space that is in modern flats and houses not so easy to find, especially as it is handy to be able to let one's tools and materials lie.

There are enough alternatives; rarely is it the case that one simply has to use a corner of the living room and clear up everything after working. A corner of the garage is very suitable except that one should not leave electronic equipment

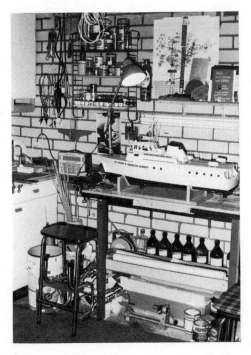

3.1. A separate workshop is ideal. A lot of tools can be stored in a permanent position.

there for long having regard to the dampness of the atmosphere – not all garages are centrally heated. Lacking a garage one mostly has a shed or hobby room. A shed has the same disadvantages as a garage and a hobby room the disadvantage that it is probably shared with the rest of the family. A loft can be ideal, but lacking anything else one can use the kitchen table or, as some do with success, a cupboard. Properly fitted out a cupboard can offer sufficient room. Actually anywhere is suitable provided one can comfortably work there. At the worst one has to clear up a little sawdust, a few bits of wood and scraps of paper, even if only to keep the lady of the house happy.

Where there is a will there is a way; everyone interested in model building will find somewhere suitable. A table 1 to $1\frac{1}{2}$ metres long by 80 cm broad is a good beginning. A good lamp is also essential and somewhere to sit; a stool is enough. The lamp should be adjustable, the sort of desk lamp that can be clamped to a desk or a table and is adjustable in any direction is ideal, but a fluourescent lamp can also give a good enough light. The size of table mentioned allows room for the tools in use and for parts that one has ready assembled. Construction drawings can be pinned to the wall.

Should one consider extra electric sockets necessary, or an extension, do bear in mind that this should be done in a professional way. If you are yourself not up to the standard, let an electrician do it. It doesn't cost much and you may spare yourself the risk of a serious shock. Later, when you consider the use of a soldering iron, a drill or even a lathe you may have to bear in mind the permissible loading on the branch.

Tools

Having found a suitable work-place plus bench or table, we should take a look in the tool box to see what we have. Although most do-it-yourselfers will have a fair selection of tools, most of them will prove too large for model construction. Some fine tools will, therefore, have to be acquired.

Usually one will have to acquire: a light hammer, a small woodsaw, small combination pliers, a brace (or even an electric drill) together with metal and wood drills (1 mm to 10 mm), a box of map pins, an instrument vice, a set of clamps, some clothes pegs, a fretsaw with blades for wood and metal, a fine hacksaw, a miniature electric drill (battery or transformer) with appropriate drill, dentists' drills, grindstones and milling tools, dentists' tools (mirror and probes), sharp-nosed half-round pliers, miniature, flat-nosed pliers, a set of screwdrivers, round nosed pliers, side cutting pliers, an electric soldering iron (about 40 Watt) with resin cored solder, a pair of straight fine-nosed pincers, a Stanley or other sort of modelling knife or scalpel with the necessary blades, chisels, instrument makers' file, instrument makers' screwdrivers, smoothing plane, a wood rasp, metal files, paint brushes in various sizes, various grades of sandpaper and, of course, scissors. Finally, such accessories as drawing pins, razor blades, pencil, ruler, a steel straight-edge, a protractor, compass, drawing pen and glue.

Of course, not everything has to be bought at one go. One can acquire things gradually – there are enough birthdays and Christmases if one but lets one's friends and family know what one wants. The tools that are essential to begin are those for cutting and sawing wood, for drilling and sanding, a few fine

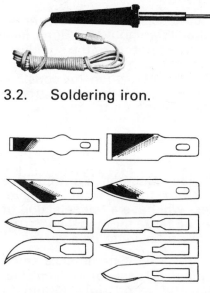

3.2.   Soldering iron.

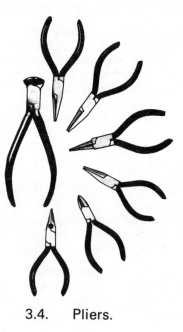

3.3.   Modelling knives.   3.4.   Pliers.

32

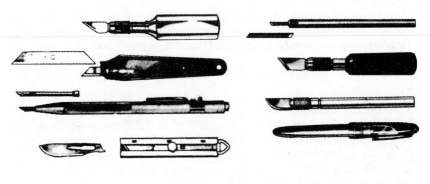

3.5. Blade holders.

3.6. Miniature drills
that can be adapted for
milling and polishing
are very handy.

screwdrivers, some pliers, and a soldering iron. Usually one
can see from the work the sort of tools that are needed. It is
only much later that one feels the need for power tools, under
which one can mention a lathe for metal and wood which, if
one can operate it, can be very useful.

Cements and glues

There are innumerable cements and glues available to the
model builder. A complete range that covers all purposes is

sold under the UHU brand. Other manufacturers supply two-component epoxy cements, some of which harden off in 4 to 15 minutes, others taking a half hour longer. Stabilit-Ultra and Stabilit-Express are well known in model building circles. These cements can be bought in virtually every model shop.

There are also enough wood glues available. Humbrol, probably better known for their model builders enamels and tools, have a special glue for balsa wood. Even the polyvvynilacetate wood glues from Gloy or Cetabever are very practical even if they do take time to harden off, in contrast to some other glues that harden in minutes. A very well known American white wood glue that hardens fast and is very strong is Titebond. Any model building shop offers choice enough, including those for plastics. Read and adhere to the instructions on the packing very carefully, especially with the cyano-acrylate cements which harden off in several seconds and form an immovable joint, but which, unfortunately, can-

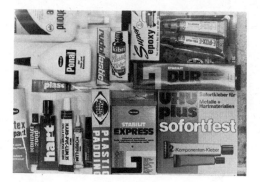

3.7. The model builder can choose from a host of different glues and cements.

not be used with wood. If one wants to know which glue or cement to use with a specific material one should consult one of the guides that various manufacturers issue.

Most model builders remain faithful to a particular glue or cement once they have found one that satisfies them. Why experiment when you know what a particular glue or cement can do? Nevertheless, it is often worthwhile trying out new sorts to see if there is an improvement.

Small tools and tubes of glue can be very satisfactorily stored in one of those angler's cases. Later the case can be used, with other small tools added, as a 'first aid' kit at the waterside. Anglers' cases are not so strong as metal tool boxes, so don't put heavy tools in one and don't pack it too full. It'll serve you far longer! For small screws, washers, rings and electronic components, those small stacked drawers used by 'do-it-yourselfers' are very handy. A hobby wall fitted with Terry clips for the larger tools can be quite a help. If possible it is worth while dropping into a hobby shop, or tool shop just to see what can be had. One can also get an idea of what it is going to cost.

Looking after tools

It is more important to know *how* tools should be stored than *where*. As far as the latter point is concerned, cool and dry are the watchwords. If metal tools remain unused for some time it is better to give them a smear of acid-free petroleum jelly or

3.8. An angler's case is an ideal thing for carrying tools and parts in.

3.9. Plastic chests of drawers for small parts and nails, etc.

vegetable oil. Wood and twist drills can be stored, standing, in a block of wood in which one has drilled holes of appropriate size. The drills should be point downwards to prevent the cutting edges being damaged. Ensure that the cutting edges are always sharp. While we are talking about drills: always drill pilot holes before drilling to size. One gets a cleaner hole and puts less load on the drills.

Chisels can be stored with the cutting edge pushed into a cork. The same can be done with wood-carving tools. Small chisels can be stuck into a piece of balsa wood. Files should be cleaned from time to time with a file card, never with a steel wire brush. And keep them free from oils and greases! Files are usually hung up in such a way that they don't contact each other and become blunted. This is also true of most other tools.

Fretsaw and small hacksaw blades can be stored very handily in pieces of plastic conduit about 10 cm long. Two rows of these tubes can be cemented together and fixed to a wooden base so that each saw has its own place. Brushes should be cleaned after use with petrol, turpentine or thinners, depending on the paint one has used. Set them to dry vertically (brush upward) in a dust-free place. Once dry they can be laid in a small box, a cigar box if you happen to know anybody who can afford cigars. Brushes of marten hair should be treated with a little acid-free petroleum jelly after cleaning. Before using brushes, dust and loose hairs should be removed by rubbing them on the hand. An empty cigar box can also be used for storing small tools and drawing material, if necessary partitioned off.

Remember, too, a metal stand or holder for the soldering iron (fire prevention). And while we are on fire prevention don't forget to keep inflammable materials and solutions well away from stoves. A small fire extinguisher (powder or foam) belongs, really, in every workshop. Electric cables and leads should be properly fitted and safe and, where necessary, fitted with an earth connection.

In general, don't let your (expensive) tools just lie around. Make a habit of tidiness. It is not only good for the model you are building, but also ensures that everything runs more smoothly and more efficiently.

Materials

One can build a model ship from wood, cardboard, plastic, aluminium, tinplate or brass, yes, even from adhesive paper tape! We will now examine the advantages and disadvantages of these materials.

Wood

A fairly obvious choice that can be obtained virtually any-where. In fact, there are many sorts that are not all equally suitable for model making. In most kits one finds balsa. It is a light and soft wood that is often used for model aeroplanes and is sold in most model shops. Deal, beech (provided it is steamed), ash, oak and lime are also suitable. The various plywoods and some of the veneers can also be used. Of course, hardwoods such as mahogany, cedar and teak, although expensive, lend themselves to model building, although they are mostly used for finishing and then only to a limited extent.

Waterproof plywood

Waterproof plywood is not difficult to work with. It can be sawn, shaped, glued and sanded. The very thin (1 mm) ply can even be cut with a knife and is especially suitable for the hull skins, decks and deckhouses. The thicker ply (from 5 mm

3.10.   This fast torpedo boat is made entirely of waterproof plywood (the author).

up) is mostly used for ribs, keels, and the stand used to support the model. It is strong and tough and absorbs but little paint. The description 'waterproof' is an indication that the laminate will not deform even in damp environments, that is to say that no damp will penetrate between the layers.

A disadvantage of ply is that it is so stiff. Where it must be formed recourse is had to water and/or steam. The damp ply has to be formed against the ribs, being held in position by pins, clamps, or nails in such a way that it can easily be freed. Once the material has thoroughly dried out it can be glued in position. In fact this is true of all materials; the surface to be glued or cemented must be really clean and dry.

Balsa wood

Balsa wood is used for innumerable purposes in model building. Because of its open structure it lends itself to cutting, planing, and sanding and it is, furthermore, easy to cement. With thicknesses below 5 mm and with the aid of steam it can be formed. A disadvantage is that because of the open porous structure it behaves like a sponge when in contact with water and swells much more than other woods. A hull that has not been properly treated can literally burst apart. Just because balsa wood is so soft it is easy to remove too much material when sanding to shape. Usually it is then better (and quicker) to make a new part instead of trying to repair the part with plastic wood, which, in any case can always be tried as a last resort. Deep scratches are often caused by the use of too coarse a sandpaper; this is no problem if a lot of material has to be removed and one can change to finer sandpaper for finishing. Balsa wood is not very strong, particularly on the sur-

3.11.   Planks of balsa.

3.12.   Strips and square sections of balsa.

faces that have been 'machined', and because it is so soft it is much more easily damaged than other types of wood. Damage can be prevented by protecting the surface with a 2 mm layer of glass fibre and polyester, which forms sufficient protection for most purposes.

A few coats of enamel on the outside surface is sufficient in some cases, the inside then receiving a couple of coats of primer. A so-called pore filler is available for balsa wood that penetrates the pores and hardens. There is no reason why it should not be used for other types of wood.

Cutting

Balsa can easily be cut along the grain, less easily across the grain. This last is more noticeable when cutting into the sides and when cutting out circles. Suddenly it becomes very

3.13. The hull and superstructure of this model fishing vessel is almost completely of balsa (Y. Götte, NL)

brittle, splinters and crumbles off along the grain, especially if the knife isn't too sharp!

One should always remember to cut or saw outside the lines unless the instructions specifically say otherwise. There remains, then, always enough material to plane or sand away. Finishing should be such that the line is just visible. A line is $\frac{1}{2}$ to 1 mm thick, and it makes quite a difference if one has shaved the line completely off on one part and let it remain on another.

If a door or window has to be cut out of balsa it is better to use a fine surgical lancet, which one can obtain in a model shop.

If one cuts towards the sides there is considerable chance of pieces splintering off. One should always cut towards where the most material is, i.e., in most cases toward the centre. With the fingers supporting both sides of the cut, draw the knife towards yourself. For short incisions some pressure is required. When a fretsaw is used very smooth edges are obtained.

In most kits the balsa has either been sawn or punched out to size so that there are less problems than we appear to suggest here. But it is worth while being aware of some of the less pleasant properties of balsa if one wants a well finished model.

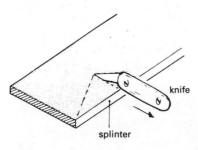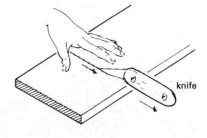

wrong   right

3.14.   Cutting so that balsa doesn't splinter.

40

3.15. In the construction of the motorship 'Helgoland' hardwoods and plywood form the major part. (C. Blankaert, B).

Balsa strip or dowel

With balsa strip or dowel there are other problems: when cutting off lengths one must work gradually round the strip until it is cut through. In this way one avoids any tendency to run out of perpendicular: care should be taken to cut and not to press, otherwise the wood tends to collapse and crumble away. The edge that has been cut can be smoothed by holding it perpendicular against a piece of glass paper held flat on the table. Care must be taken that the wood is perfectly perpendicular otherwise one side will be sanded away and not the other.

Other sorts of wood

If we treated other types of wood so extensively as we have balsa we would need a few more chapters. Balsa is the most used and therefore receives the most extensive treatment. All other woods are tougher, harder and, above all, heavier than balsa. Which is why cutting is not so simple, unless very thin material is involved. Sawing is certainly more accurate and a

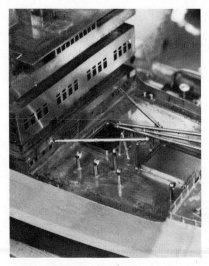

3.16. Detail of the deck of a passenger ship where thin brass is used.

3.17. Brass tube and wire used for railings and masts.

better finish can be obtained when planing, filing or sanding. Hardwoods are not so porous as balsa and do not splinter so readily. One does not need a layer of polyester to protect it against damage, although this can be done if one desires. It depends on the construction of the ship. In building a ship the weight of wood is not really important; in practice one has to add weight to get the boat to float on the water-line.

Advice: If it is in any way possible use hardwood and finish it off smoothly. You will find it much more pleasant to work with than balsa and that, furthermore, it is easier to obtain a good finish. At first sight balsa seems the easier material, but seems and is are different things.

Metals

If one has little or no experience in metal working it is best to make as little use of it as possible in building model ships. For other purposes metal is useful and sometimes indispensable. This is true mostly of the fittings, where bronze, copper, lead and aluminium are often used. Tinplate is sometimes used but it rusts rather quickly. Raw material is usually turned on a lathe by the more experienced model builder. An advantage of metal is that with good tools and the necessary know-how one can produce a very nice finish. Accessories can be 'cleanly' finished and are often sprayed instead of brush painted.

Some model builders have even built the entire hull of metal, usually with tinplate or bronze, which just like in real ships, is cut into plates and soldered together, (in the real thing welded). One real problem is to make the hull water-tight. It is no easy matter! Bronze, copper and tinplate are readily soldered and once one has the necessary experience one can achieve a good deal.

3.18.   This model of the old Russian warship Oktyabrskaya Revolutsia is constructed of metal. The ship won third prize in the 1975 European Championships. (H. Schwarzer, DDR).

3.19.   Ready-to-use plastic hull.

Copper and bronze wire is, amongst other things, used to make railings, masts and imitation oil and steam pipes. Tin-plate is often used to make companion ways, deck-houses, funnels, small flat parts (such as doors, hatches and manhole covers) and gun parts in warships. To prevent rust it must be painted. If large surfaces have to be soldered there is considerable chance of deformation.

Aluminium is easier to obtain than copper, bronze and tin-plate and is, furthermore, cheaper than the two first-named and, above all, rust-proof. It can readily be cemented with epoxy cements and it is possible to solder it – with a cadmium-zinc alloy. That way one gets a hard-soldered joint, although a soft solder is obtainable. Try the do-it-yourself shop for these things. Aluminium can be easily sawn, drilled and sanded: it can be finished off beautifully smooth and can be obtained in a variety of thicknesses. In ship model building thicknesses from $\frac{1}{2}$ mm are perfectly usable.

3.20.   The light cruiser Nürnberg is constructed entirely of thin display cardboard and balsa wood covered with a thin layer of polyester (the author).

44

Copper can be used for the same purposes as bronze and aluminium. It is malleable, but is mostly used in those places where a strong joint is needed or support is required, although it is softer than bronze. It is relatively expensive. Just like bronze, it solders well.

Lead is mostly used to 'trim' the boat once it is finished, that is to say, to balance the hull so that it floats vertically in the water and doesn't capsize. Trimming is the last thing to be done, once everything is built in – including motors, batteries and radio control. Sometimes fittings are of cast lead (especially with American kits). The finish is not so good as with plastic, and lead bends easily and is prone to breakage.

In a very few cases zinc is also used in model building. It solders perfectly but is stiff and heavy.

Plastic

Some kits contain a complete plastic hull. The material, usually styrene (acrylonitrile butadiene styrene), lends itself well to cementing, but sawing and cutting are fairly difficult. To remove a piece from such a hull one can better use a hot soldering iron as knife.

Plastic is also used for the superstructure; complete deck-houses and other accessories can be expected in a kit. Polyester, usually used in combination with a reinforcement such as

3.21. The hull and superstructure of this English F 51 Ashanti Class destroyer is of impregnated paper. Here a detail aft (D. Brown, GB).

glass fibre, is another matter. The resin is mixed with a catalyst or hardener, or combination thereof and allowed to harden. Polyester is almost exclusively used in the construction of the hull; once hardened it is strong and tough and can easily be sanded. A smooth surface is quickly obtained which lends itself to a fine paint finish.

One can buy powder which when mixed with the resin and other ingredients makes an excellent filler. It hardens off within a half hour and is easy to work.

Model shops have a variety of plastic sheet with the appropriate cements and one can usually obtain professional advice from them.

Anyone who has ever built a model from a plastic kit will have an impression of what working with plastic is like. Just like metal, plastic has the advantage that a smooth surface can be obtained and that it doesn't splinter. Parts come straight and flat from the sheet which makes it especially suitable for deckhouses.

Paper and cardboard

Stiff paper and cardboard ($\frac{1}{2}$, 1, $1\frac{1}{2}$, or 2 mm thick) is also an excellent material. It is easy to cut with scissors or knife and is easy to glue. Even a complete hull can be made of cardboard and provided it is strengthened in the right places both longitudinally and with ribs, it can be particularly strong. It needs to be impregnated with either shellac or pore-filler, or with clear varnish. Finishing with polyester is, of course, also possible.

Cardboard ships can be sailed; even radio control equipment can be built in. Under normal conditions there is not the slightest danger of a drop of water getting in. The superstructure can also be made of cardboard or stiff paper; the paint will make it sufficiently waterproof.

A disadvantage of paper is that it cannot be sanded. If long unsupported strips are used it tends to cockle or bend.

Finally, gummed paper (tape) can be used. To form a hull, one builds up a number of layers in various directions over a frame of ribs. Having built up at least six layers one can finish off with filler and paint or polyester.

4 Constructing the hull

Having gained enough knowledge from the foregoing to start work, an attempt will be made to give a fairly extensive description of a number of construction methods and the problems commonly met with. No single type of hull is described, simply because there are so many that it would be impossible to describe them all in a single book. Once one has mastered the principles one can build any sort of hull one wishes. It is assumed that one has a construction drawing so that the design already exists, at least on paper. With the aid of the drawing one can build the model, but first a few words about the drawing.

There is a construction drawing for every ship. One can obtain such drawings of the real ship through the company operating the ship or the yards where the ship was built. Because there is so much detail on the drawings that is, initially at least, of little use, they give a rather cluttered impression. With a kit one usually gets a model drawing which draughtsmen have redrawn from the original and have omitted all the, for the model builder, unnecessary detail. Such a drawing is more 'readable' for the amateur and is the most suitable for a beginner.

Drawings can also be obtained from model builders' clubs (a list is given at the end of the book).

The construction drawing

The construction drawing usually comprises three main parts:
a). a complete side view of the ship, sometimes with horizontal lines parallel to the waterline (CWL or *Construction Water Line*) sometimes known as the lines plan.
b). a cross-section or a body plan, sometimes both.
c). a plan viewed from both above and below in the same drawing.
Together these drawings form a general plan, an example of which is given in Fig. 4.1.

47

The construction drawing is, of course, two dimensional and one must learn to see it three dimensionally in order to recognise, measure and construct the individual parts. Where the drawing is in the scale 1:1, one can transfer the measurements direct from drawing to building material. Where another scale is used one will have to reduce or enlarge every dimension to the same ratio.

In the cross-section one half shows the construction from amidships to stern, the other half, from amidships to bow. The body or rib structure is, therefore only half drawn and to obtain a complete structure one must rotate the drawing about the centre line.

Figure and letters in the plan refer to the lines plan. Check them carefully and mark on the keel the point where the ribs will come. The plan view is usually directly below the side view so that the plan and side views of a part are in line with one another. Some of the large details are also separately drawn in the same way.

It is as well to study the drawing carefully before beginning construction; in fact one ought to know it by heart before beginning. If one is building from a kit one should remove no more from the box than is necessary to complete a specific detail or part, otherwise one is likely to lose bits.

Should one be using a construction drawing it is a good idea to make one or more copies before beginning. One needn't then be afraid of cutting into the drawing when cutting out parts, or of getting glue or cement onto it. The original can best be mounted on a piece of board and hung on the wall where it will maintain its original condition. Don't forget a drawing has to last a long time – several years is no exception.

Where lines must be transferred to the construction material do this carefully and with the help of good carbon paper. One should always cut outside the lines. Excess material can always be removed; too little can scarcely ever be made good.

Scales

The actual measurements of the real ship are often also found on the drawings. If the scale is 1:20 (as in Fig. 4.1.) then should

48

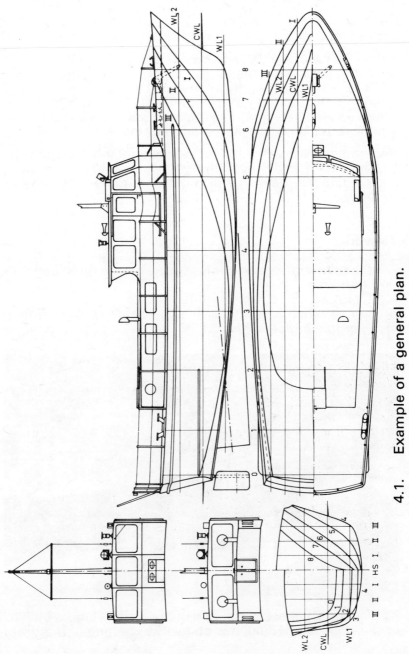

4.1.   Example of a general plan.

49

the length of the actual boat be 20 metres, the model will be 1 metre long.

Everything will be 1/20th the size of the real thing. Should one be building a 300 metre tank to a scale of 1:100 the model will be 3 metres long. Apart from transport to the water where can you keep such a thing at home? Think, therefore, always in scales and when acquiring a model kit bear in mind the space you have for both building it and storing it.

Remember always first study, then cut out, offer the parts up to each other, and if everything fits, cement together. Most kits contain instructions which one should read and attempt to follow.

To work

For the moment we can confine ourselves to three construction methods:
a). the bread and butter method,
b). frames with a covering, as in a real ship (plank-on-frame),
c). a complete plastic hull.

4.2.   This Duchess of Holland of the Norfolk Line is built to a scale of 1:300, it is about 170 cm long (J.B.B. Fick, NL).

a) Bread and butter construction

With this method pre-sawn planks are screwed and glued together in such a sequence that a hull is constructed that fully agrees with the drawing. If one is using a kit the pre-sawn planks will either be available or in any case ready drawn. If they are neither pre-sawn nor drawn one will have to transfer the contours of the hull onto wood. Make sure that the planks are free of knots, otherwise it is almost impossible to obtain a good finish.

The planks should be longer than the dimensions given on the drawing in order to leave material for correcting the shape during finishing and for clamping during the work.

Working method

Assume that there are ten equally thick planks needed (if possible make them as thick as the distance between the horizontal lines). Set one on top of the other – these planks are now the same height as the centre line of the hull on the drawing (bulwarks, etc. excepted).

4.3. This model of a French warship is constructed on the sandwich principle (F. Coquet, F).

Draw in the thickness of the planks on the cross-sectional body drawing ensuring that they are parallel to the base and perpendicular to the centre-line. Number the planks using Roman numerals (Fig. 4.4.). A number of intersections have now been formed between the base lines (plank thicknesses) and the centre-line and the contours of the hull. The distance between the centre-line and the hull contour determines the shape of the hull at that point.

Beginning with the lowest plank (I), a centre line is now drawn longitudinally. The sides of the plank must be as straight as possible to allow the use of a set square. Using dividers the distances (A) between ribs (taken from the side view) are now stepped out (see Fig. 4.5.). Fig. 4.5. shows also how the distance between centre-line and hull, perpendicular to the centre-line, is determined. The arrow points towards the bow. The rib lines are now drawn using a set-square and are numbered with the same code as the side view. Other planks are now dealt with in the same manner.

Taking the distance between centre-line (C) and rib 7, beginning with the lowest plank I. If we work from fore to aft, this

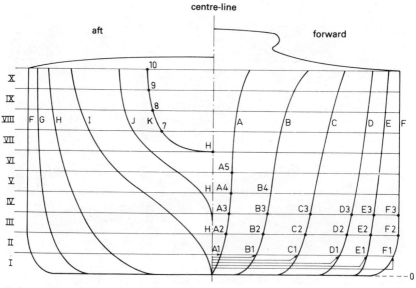

4.4.   Cross-section fore and aft.

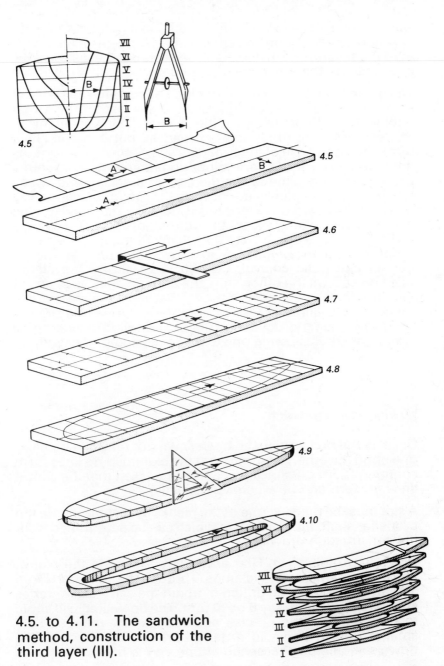

4.5

4.5

4.6

4.7

4.8

4.9

4.10

VII
VI
V
IV
III
II
I

4.5. to 4.11. The sandwich method, construction of the third layer (III).

53

will be the distance H − A¹ (Fig. 4.4.). Taking the compasses one marks intersections on either side of the centre-line for rib A. At the second line on the plank one sets out the distance H − B¹ and at the third line H − C¹, and so on.

The same is done for the other side i.e., the after part of the ship. So doing, a series of crosses have been drawn that outline the form of the hull at the level of the lowest plank. In this example one rib, F, is the broadest, but in some ships more than one rib is of the broadest size. Once all the crosses have been drawn they are joined together with a smoothly curving line. This line forms the circumference along which one will saw. All planks are now dealt with in the same way and are then sawn out. Once this is done one can saw out the centre of each plank (except the bottom, of course), leaving a wall thickness of about 2 cm (Fig. 4.10). Removing the centre is not so much for weight saving as to create space for motor, battery and radio control, etc. Fig. 4.11. shows the planks piled one above the other; here the upper plank has been left whole to form a deck but in a model that will be sailed it would be cut out to allow access to the interior. A well fitting but removable superstructure is added later to make everything water tight, but allowing one to get to the equipment within.

Making the 'sandwich':

Once all the hull parts have been sawn out they can be piled one upon the other, ensuring that the extended rib lines form continuous lines. Especial care must be taken that the centre lines at stern and bow coincide exactly.

A slot must be made in one of the planks to accommodate the propellor shaft, the position of which can be determined from the construction drawing.

Don't start gluing yet. First accurately assemble the planks and make them fast with clamps. Through the solid parts fore and aft a hole must be drilled of about the same diameter as standard dowelling, say 8 or 10 mm. The dowelling will serve to hold parts in the precise position during gluing. Use a smaller drill to begin in order to prevent splintering. The dowels should be sharpened at one end to make it easier to

54

drive through the holes. Never use metal dowels as these may become proud during planing and sanding and give rise to difficulties.

One begins with the base and works toward the deck. The faces of planks I and II are evenly covered with waterproof wood glue and are brought together over the dowelling. If necessary, use *copper* nails or screws to clamp them but ensure that they are far enough from the outer edge not to become proud during planing and sanding.

Once the glue has set, the third plank can be treated in the same way, and so on until one has the rough form of the hull – only the rough form, because there is still an awful lot of planing and sanding to do.

As a check during sanding and planing one makes a number of templates, each having the shape of the hull at a particular rib. The templates can be made of stiff card and can be set against the hull to check the shape. When no daylight can be seen the hull is of the right shape at that point along its length.

When sanding use the whole hand and let it follow the form of the hull. Begin with coarse sandpaper and work through to the finest. Dry sandpaper is preferred to wet as balsa can absorb a great deal of water. One can treat the hull with a thin layer of polyester resin (more about this later in the chapter).

At this point one can give the hull a coat of primer, if necessary using a pore-filler.

Plank-on-frame method

The plank-on-frame system is the most common in model building as well as in actual ship building. The system makes use of a number of ribs that are positioned in sequence on a keel and held in place by stringers. This rib cage is then covered with a skin of some thickness – in model building 0.5 to 1 or 1.5 mm.

One needs to bear in mind how the motor(s) are to be built in as this often necessitates removing ribs or parts of ribs to create the necessary space. Neither must one forget the propeller shaft. It is easy to make changes before everything is glued in position – thereafter, less so. Always check and fit,

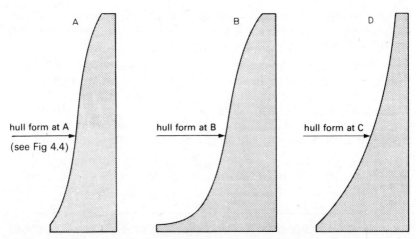

A · B · D

hull form at A
(see Fig 4.4)

hull form at B

hull form at C

4.12. A few templates derived from the rib contours (see Fig. 4.4) used to check the shape of the hull.

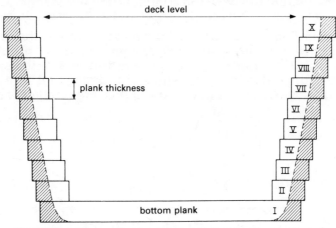

deck level

plank thickness

X
IX
VIII
VII
VI
V
IV
III
II
I

bottom plank

4.13. Cross-section of a bread-and-butter hull, the shaded parts are sanded away to give the final form of the hull.

therefore. The plank-on-frame method has some advantages compared with the bread and butter system. Once the skin has been added and everything is watertight one only needs to sand and paint; planing and filing are usually unnecessary. Further, there is more room for motor, etc, and also more places on the ribs to make everything fast, and, as a final

56

point, one has a more professional hull. There are, of course, also disadvantages:- especially with large models where there is a tendency for the keel to warp when the stringers or the side supports are not sumultaneously fitted. Forming and tensioning the (wet or steamed) skin segments can also be troublesome. Furthermore, the ribs can be set skew on the keel, especially with a curved keel.

One starts, in any case, by studying the construction drawing. It is advisable to build (literally) direct on the construction drawing – at least, on a copy of it. Where possible the model should be built upside down, with the keel uppermost. In the event that the sides are curved, one makes supports to take up the space between ribs and drawing so that the ribs fully carry the form of the ship.

Where this is not possible, the keel should be fastened to the bench using nails or screws. Set the ribs in position but don't cement them yet; it may be necessary to take them off again. Join the ribs together with stringers, for which there are usually recesses in the outside edges of the ribs. Work on both sides simultaneously and from aft to fore (or the other way about), provided the bow is not too curved. In the latter case one has to steam the stringers a little longer at that point in order to make them more flexible. Setting up and pre-tensioning these strips is the most difficult part. It is a bit like trying to manage a bag of worms! If everything goes good one proceeds with the following ribs, always working on both sides simultaneously. When the stringers are dry they can be glued in place.

If most of the ribs are in contact with the work bench they can be made fast to the keel with pins or nails. Ensure that these

4.14. Apart from providing the shape, ribs strengthened by stringers also give the hull its strength.

4.15. Jason twins. In the foreground a model built by the bread-and-butter method, in the background one with a rib construction.

are perpendicular to the keel. The ribs are both vertically and horizontally in the right position. If extra stringers have to be added minor faults can be corrected. If the ribs are now viewed along the top at eye level they should be level and straight (unless the curve of the deck doesn't allow it). Once the cement is hard the keel and ribs can be lifted from the bench and set in the proper position, if necessary with support blocks to support the rather fragile framework.

This method is all right provided the keel is straight over most of its length. In other cases one has to choose the best method of finishing the hull; perhaps with it upside down, perhaps with it the right way up. In any case, once the framework is ready for covering with the skin segments one has to work

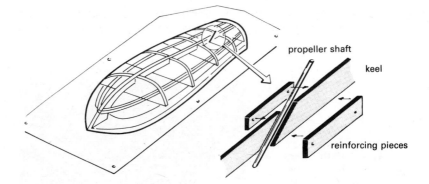

propeller shaft

keel

reinforcing pieces

4.16.   Building with the keel upward.

4.17. A model of the Tirpitz during construction. The ribbed hull is clad with polyester and is in two parts to facilitate transport (M.S.V. Schwelm, BRD).

upside down in order to make the underside water-tight. One always works from the keel to bulwarks when cladding the rib cage. (Fig. 4.18.).

Before the ribs are glued in position it is as well to make the slot for the propeller shaft. It is very difficult to drill this accurately at a later stage. (Fig. 4.16.).

The ribs one finds in a kit are usually pre-sawn. If not, one has to transfer the outlines onto the wood. A fretsaw is best for cutting out. In about 90% of models the ribs are of 5 to 8 mm plywood. The keel may be of hardwood but is sometimes of balsa. The keel may also be built up of several parts, and is sometimes no thicker than the ribs.

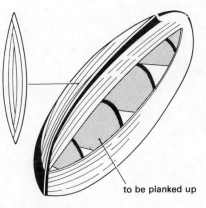

to be planked up

4.18.   One works from the keel toward the deck.

The pre-sawn grooves ensure the parts fit accurately and firmly together. Before covering the hull one must check as to whether there is sufficient room for motor(s) and propeller shaft. In fact one should really build the ship around the motor!

The skin

The ribs can be covered in various ways. In kits the skin segments are usually pre-drawn on the wood. If not, one must transfer in the usual way. The skin segments are usually long strips that should be checked for fit before they are glued to the ribs. Where they are too stiff one must either steam them or wet them.

The thinner the wood the easier it is to bend, but the more vulnerable it is, unless one adds a coating of polyester. The skin of the hull is usually of waterproof ply. For thicker skins

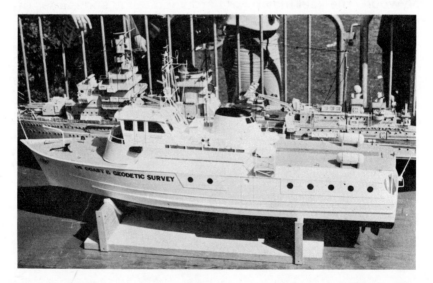

4.19.   A model of the Wesselina, an American Coast and Geodetic Survey vessel. It is completely of balsa on a ribbed hull (see Fig. 4.14). The funnel is of plastic sheet. The Sterling Models version of the Caltex 'Lumba-Lumba' served as basis for this design.

10 mm broad by 5 mm thick beech may be used. The cementing must be good otherwise problems tend to arise, with a leaky hull.

One can use pins, nails, clothes pegs or elastic bands to hold the parts in place while one is working. They should be left in position until the cement is dry, and then removed when they get in the way of further work. Strictly this is only true for nails or screws unless a permanent fastening is required, in which case a small drift should be used to punch the heads below the surface. The resultant hollow can be filled with plastic wood or filler.

4.20. The hull of the tugboat Aegir is constructed of plywood ribs with beechwood stringers covered with a layer of polyester (H.K.J.v.d. Bussche, NL).

Provision for propeller shaft and rudder

From the construction drawing one can see at which places the motor(s) and rudders have to be positioned and, therefore, at which places holes must be drilled in the hull. It depends on the type of ship as to whether there is more than one screw or rudder. Most ships are driven from the stern, so that is where the thrust mechanism must be fitted. Occasionally one finds a ship with bow thrusters, but these are usually drilling platforms, ferry boats, ice breakers, etc. Bow thrusters are also used for steering, which is a reason for fitting them on some models. How they are mounted will be dealt with in Chapter 9.

The holes in the hull are carefully drilled with a brace. Always drill a pilot hole. Take especial care with the direction and the angle with respect to the keel. Correct where necessary. Later one can make the hole larger so that the propeller shaft has sufficient room and even some play. The hole for the rudder shaft should be a fairly tight fit. Where necessary, i.e., if the hull is thin at that point, one should strengthen the area round the hole for the propeller shaft. With bread and butter built hulls there is always sufficient 'meat'.

4.21. Detail of a model freighter, the single screw of which is made of bronze.

4.22. Each propeller with its own rudder. The rudders of the heavy cruiser Admiral Scheer are set obliquely under the stern. The model can execute no less than 32 functions. (H. Müster, BRD).

A single propeller shaft is fitted centrally; if there are two these are fitted equidistant from the centre-line. If there is one propeller there is usually only one rudder. Where there are more propellers it may be that each propeller has its own rudder, which greatly increases the steering capability. Here again, it depends on the type of ship. There are even ships with three or four propellers. Consider warships: battleships and aircraft carriers usually have more than two propellers with an equal number of rudders – and in models that are going to be sailed they need to work (See Fig. 3.18.).

Having drilled the necessary holes one must exercise some patience before getting on with the actual mounting of the propeller shaft and rudder. First the unfinished hull must be planed (bread and butter built hulls) or sanded (plank-on-frame).

Combinations of bread and butter and plank-on-frame methods

Apart from the pure bread and butter and plank-on-frame methods there are also combinations of these: sometimes one comes across kits where stem and stern are built up from ribs covered with strips or laths and the midship is built according to the sandwich method. The three parts are then fitted together to make a whole.

With the plank-on-frame method one also encounters stringers (longitudinal members) as well as ribs. They add strength longitudinally and make the whole thing look a bit like an egg box. (Fig. 4.23.). The ribs are usually solid which means that they must be borne in mind when it comes to situating the motor(s) and batteries. Sometimes the bow and stern are simply blocks that once cemented, only need to be planed and sanded. Usually one ends up with a piece of grain that needs to be properly filled. Impregnated cardboard is also sometimes used for the skin of the hull. It is easy to shape but the strength leaves something to be desired, something that can be remedied by a coating of polyester.

Most ribs come ready to use in the kit but there are also some that are made up of as many as four separate parts. After

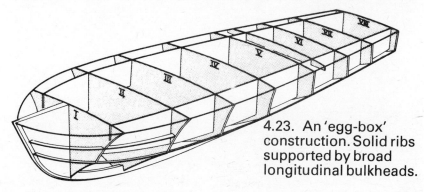

4.23. An 'egg-box' construction. Solid ribs supported by broad longitudinal bulkheads.

sawing them out one has to glue them together, an operation that requires care if one is not to end up with a dented hull.

Sometimes a ribbed model is not covered with longitudinal strips but with diagonal ones. Very occasionally one meets a case where the strips are laid in the vertical direction.

Clinker built constructions are also met with. All in all countless combinations but in virtually every case there is a pattern in the building method.

At this point one can think about finishing the hull. Initially with a rasp and thereafter with coarse and fine sandpaper. It goes without saying that one uses the tools needed for each particular case. If the hull is smooth, sandpaper will be enough; a roughly finished hull (sandwich) will call for a plane (or rasp).

Once the hull has been smoothed one can think about filling any hollows or gaps in it. Use a good filler, the two-component ones are the best (plastic metal) which one can acquire from the car specialists. It adheres well and hardens fast. When the filler is dry one can sand again, repeating the operation until one has a perfectly shaped hull. Where appropriate one can now add the stabilisers – make certain that they are firmly glued in place.

Stabilisers are longitudinal 'bilge keels' that are fitted perpendicularly to the hull and are primarily for lateral stability. (Fig. 4.24). They are fitted to both sides and vary in length from a quarter to a half of the length of the ship. Once they are firmly set in position one can give the hull its first coat of

4.24. The stabilisers under the hull of the tugboat Moorcock can be clearly seen (HMBC exhibition).

64

primer. This coat protects the hull against minor damage, oil spots in the workshop, and damp. A balsa construction should also be strengthened by several layers of pore filler, which can be bought in every model shop. It makes the surface of the balsa harder and also fills the pores so that the paint brushes on nicely and is not sucked up with the first stroke.

An internal coat of paint or glass fibre polyester resin is also essential. Should water ever enter the hull this protective coat ensures that the wood is not immediately saturated. Many a hull (especially balsa hulls) have split in consequence of a lack of paint on the inside. It is not the most pleasant sight in the world to see your expensive radio control equipment floating around . . .!

With the rib cage method less material needs to be removed. It only needs to be sanded smooth, and the corners rounded off, where necessary, and to fill as needed. Once it is dry one can sand off and once again give a coat of primer both internally and externally.

4.25. Anchor and hawse-hole on a freighter.

4.26. When the anchor is on deck we can sometimes see an open hawse-hole (G.Rudolph, BRD).

4.27. Eyelets as portholes, they are filled with cement to make them waterproof.

Completing the hull

The hawse holes can now be drilled on both sides of the hull. These serve, in the first instance, to let the anchor chain through but they also house the shaft of the anchor itself. One can see from the construction drawing precisely where they must be drilled. With some warships there are also hawse holes aft. The holes run through the hull and open out on the deck. First mark off the positions accurately and then using a fine drill, drill through from deck to the side of the hull. After drilling they must be reamed out to the proper size. The edge is sometimes finished off with wire or three-ply.

Sometimes the hole is squared off to form an exact fit for the anchor shaft. This can be done with a chisel. With the sandwich construction there is enough meat for this; with rib construction one needs to fit a wooden block where the hawse hole will be before cutting into the hull. With some ships the anchors lie on deck in which case the bulwarks are suitably indented. The old German warships of the Atlantik class had this aft.

66

4.28. Smooth lines when viewed along the side (J. Mireau, BRD).

Most ships have port-holes and, should the kit contain nothing to make these, they can be very successfully imitated with eyelets. Various sizes can be obtained from the ironmonger's or the 'do-it-yourself' shop. Actual holes can be made, of course, but transparent glass or plastic must be fitted behind the hole. A good cement is needed, preferably a contact glue. The holes must in any case be watertight, a subject that will be dealt with in Chapter 8.

4.29. The cruiser Nürnberg which is constructed of carton cardboard and polyester has a top speed of 5 km/hr (the author).

The complete plastic hull

With some kits we get a complete, ready-to-use plastic hull of styrene or a.b.s. That ready-to-use only refers to the shape of the hull that we find in the kit; there is still an awful lot of cutting, drilling and cementing before it is really ready.

Usually the hull is too high and some of the plastic round the sides has to be cut away to attain the right measurements, and this is just what turns out to be difficult in practice. The plastic is tough and the use of a sharp knife is not only hazardous to the craft but also to hands and body. The bow of a fretsaw turns out not to be quite long enough, which causes the cut to deviate from the straight and narrow, and what is more, the heat of sawing tends to cause the sawcut to seal up behind the blade. If it is thermoplastic, one has to saw very slowly with a coarse blade.

One way is to use a soldering iron, the (old) bit of which has been filed to form a knife. If one starts well above the requisite height one will find the iron cuts like a hot knife through butter. Once the material has cooled the edge can be finished off with file and sandpaper. Try to avoid a hill and valley effect along the line. With the eye in line with the bulwark one should see a straight line, apart from any natural curvature, which should be smoothly executed. Above all do not take off too much material. When the line is barely visible check and check again with the drawing so as to be absolutely certain of what you are doing. If you take too much off you can never put it back on again, so be extra careful as you approach the line. It is also well worth while practising on a bit of waste material to get an idea of how fast one files the material away.

Once the hull has reached the point where it agrees with the drawing, one can cement in place the bulkheads (usually three or four) that come with the kit. Usually there are also some struts, either to support the deck or for the motor. It is also as well to ensure that radio receiver and batteries have their own floors. The next thing to do is to drill the holes for propeller shaft and rudder.

Let us look at the example of polyester cladding in more detail: we will need the following ingredients:

a) resin (to be had in various size tins up to 1 kg).
b) appropriate hardener and accelerator (or catalyst).

68

c) pigment (in powder form)
d) glass fibre mat.

One will also need a small plastic bucket, or an old pan or suchlike, a scale with which one can read off to a $\frac{1}{2}$ gramme and brushes (preferably old ones). Finally one will need a bottle of brush cleaner suitable for resin products or a mixture of 2 parts water, one part acetone and one part trichlorethylene.

These things can be bought at any do-it-yourself shop or at one specialising in water-sport articles. Glass fibre mat is a flexible, hairy mat which is easy to divide and from which threads can be pulled. Its thickness varies from $\frac{1}{2}$ to 1 mm. The pan or bucket that you are going to use should have sides high enough to prevent spillage when stirring and should be large enough to hold as much of the mixture as can be worked in one go. On average a boat of 1 metre with a beam of 20 cm and a height of about 10 cm will take about 1 kg of resin. The glass mat is bought by the square metre, 1 being enough for a boat of the dimensions just mentioned, if only one layer is applied. If you are careful you will probably have enough left over for the inside. For our purpose one layer is enough to give a strength comparable to that of a ready-to-use plastic hull, even if only using cardboard (of $\frac{1}{2}$ to 1 mm) as a mould.

The work

Use a well ventilated room without naked flames and *do not smoke.* Polyester usually comes as a resin with which two more ingredients, the hardener and the accelerator, must be mixed. Sometimes the accelerator is already mixed in with the resin and one only needs to add the hardener, which makes life easier. In any case mixing isn't as difficult as it seems.

The amount of hardener and accelerator that is required is prescribed by the manufacturer, usually by maximum and minimum percentages. Supposing the percentages are given as 1 – 4% hardener and 1 – 4% accelerator. The more that is added the faster the resin hardens off – but against that, the less the time we have to apply it so don't choose too high a percentage. If you work too close to one or other of the limits you run the danger that inaccuracies in measurement (you are not using laboratory equipment) will make the whole mixture unusable. At less than 1% the resin will never harden off while at too high a percentage the resin will harden too rapidly with consequent cracking and the generation of heat. For safety choose a percentage somewhere in the middle and if it then turns out that you have used 3.1 % instead of $2\frac{1}{2}$ % (which you will never find out, incidentally) no harm will be done. However, the same error of 0.6 % at 4 %, giving you a 4.6 % mixture will guarantee you a crackle-finished hull!

Put the mixing pan on the scale and note its weight, $35\frac{1}{2}$ grammes, for example. Round off the calculated amount of resin (for easier measurement), if you have calculated 480 grammes make it 500, so add resin to the pan until it reads 500 + $35\frac{1}{2}$ = $535\frac{1}{2}$ grammes. Now add $2\frac{1}{2}$ % hardener, that is, $2\frac{1}{2}$ x 5 = $12\frac{1}{2}$ grammes, bringing the total weight up to 548 grammes and stir the mixture thoroughly but slowly. Stirring too fast creates air bubbles and you don't want that.

4.30 The Duchess of Holland, a heavy and stable model. Completely clad in polyester (J.B.B. Fick, NL)

4.31 So many hulls, so many types of ship; at exhibitions and competitions one has the opportunity to admire the work of fellow enthusiasts (HMBC, The Hague).

Once the hardener is thoroughly mixed add 12½ grammes of accelerator bringing the weight up to 560½ grammes and stir again thoroughly but slowly.

Always add the hardener first and then the accelerator, never the other way around and never let hardener and accelerator come into contact with each other. In both events an explosion and/or poisonous gases can result. Should you prefer to work in volumes rather than weights you can always do so. Returning to our example one can add to 500 cc of resin, 12½ cc of hardener and 12½ cc of accelerator. If you don't have a good scale it is naturally simpler to work with measuring beakers, but more things are made dirty that later will have to be cleaned.

Once the mixture is ready it will start to harden off so you will have to go to work fairly quickly. Don't let anyone distract you and put off that cup of tea for a little while. Within about half an hour you must have used up the whole mixture. The actual hardening time is very temperature-dependent and while the resin will take days to harden off in an unheated shed, it will take only 12 to 24 hours at room temperature.

Everything must be made ready beforehand so that you don't have to go hunting for tools, etc. Even the glass fibre can be cut to size beforehand. Try the pieces 'dry' against the hull allowing for 2 – 5 mm overlap. Cover a part of the hull well with resin (it can be quite thick) and stick the glass fibre mat on the hull. Now use the brush to dab resin into the glass fibre; don't brush on because this will displace the fibres. The complete hull is consequently covered with glass fibre and resin. One must work thoroughly around the corners but always with a dabbing motion and always in one direction.

The addition of pigment or colouring may not exceed 5 % of the total weight of resin in the case of powders and 10 % in the case of pastes. If you use pastes avoid some American sorts that contain a kind of wax that makes the bonding with the following layer very difficult.

The final layer is a layer of polyester without glass fibre. Just as with painting, the base must be carefully filled and sanded. There is a powder available that when mixed with resin, hardener and accelerator, makes a kind of filler that hardens off and can be worked within a quarter of an hour.

The final coat may be followed by a second very thin coat, the resin always being prepared as described. The last coat can also be used to strengthen decks, deckhouses, etc., and be in the final colour. Use a thin coat of porefiller in advance (with cardboard or balsa) and after hardening sand off. Always give the resin 12 to 24 hours to thoroughly harden off. It may seem hard, but that is only the outer surface. One has to give it the stated time. The addition of colouring may delay the hardening process but one can counteract this by raising the ambient temperature or by adding a couple of drops more hardener. Take care that the temperature isn't too high and that not all too great temperature differences arise in the structure. If you have never worked with polyester before it is well worthwhile making a few trial attempts with small quantities and small blocks of various sorts of wood so that you learn to judge the bonding properties.

Any fillers should be added after the hardener and accelerator. One has about 20 to 30 minutes before the resin begins to gel. When it does, one should stop work, otherwise there is a danger of lumpiness. Ensure that the glass fibre is in good contact with the hull or one will get air bubbles and blisters under the final coat which are very difficult to remove once the resin is hard.

WARNING: The presence of fire is extremely dangerous when using resin products. Good ventilation is essential and don't handle the bottles of hardener and accelerator roughly (don't shake them). They are made with a peroxide base and are usually poisonous when used internally (swallowed); they can react explosively when unwisely handled. Don't let the mixture become damp; this will cause air bubbles and interfere with the hardening.

5 Propeller shaft and rudder

One can now fit propeller shaft and rudder. It is usual to glue a bronze tube at the place where the rudder shaft passes through, the upper end of which should come well above the water line. The rudder post, the upper end of which should be threaded and the lower end of which carries the rudder, is pushed through the tube with a little grease or oil.

It is as well to glue some strengthening round the rudder hole right away. The hole is usually vertical but in some warships the rudder shaft is slanted in relation to the hull (see Fig. 4.22), but these are exceptions which are immediately seen in the construction drawing.

The thread of the rudder shaft extends a little above the end of the tube and a nut is screwed on so that the shaft has just enough play to allow the rudder to turn smoothly. A cross-arm is then fitted on the shaft (Fig. 5.1) and made fast. To this is fitted a rod of the requisite length. A special link can be used (obtainable from model shops) that is not only easy to fit but also allows the length to be adjusted. Otherwise one just bends the rod (Fig. 5.2). The other end of the rod is connected to the servo, care being taken to keep the rod straight.

Fig. 5.3. is an example of how a rudder system can be fitted.

The propeller shaft

Before fitting the propeller shaft and its tube one can best look at what has come with the kit. What type is it, how long, and can the thing be dis-assembled? A bare tube within which the shaft turns and a propeller that is either pressed on or moulded on is virtually useless. The best types are those with a bearing at each end. The in-board bearing is sometimes a ball-bearing type which is a press fit in the tube, often with a vertical oil tube or grease point. The outboard bearing is usually a self lubricating synthetic one (nylon). They are more expensive but turn easier because they are lubricated and only have two bearing points (Fig. 5.4). The outboard end of the shaft is threaded – M2, M3, M4, etc. These are metric sizes in which the figure indicates the size in millimetres although M2 and M4 propellers can be used satisfactorily on 2 and 4BA shafts. Offering up the shaft and tube allows one to judge the

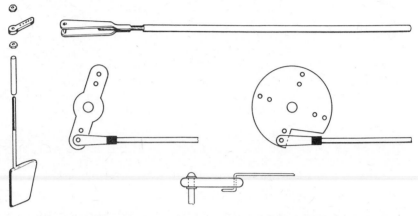

5.1 Construction of rudder, rudder shaft and steering arm.

5.2. Construction of the steering arm clevis and its connection to the servo.

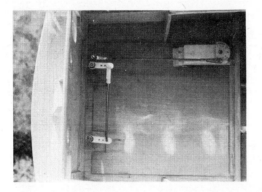

5.3. Twin rudders connected to a single servo. The rudders are equidistant on the (white) plastic steering arm and are in the straight ahead position.

position of the motor in the ship. It is as well to allow sufficient room in the motor compartment.

Propeller shafts can be obtained in various lengths which allows some flexibility in siting the motor. A good relationship between motor and shaft makes for a model that sails well, provided the same care is taken with other factors, but more of this anon. Ships with a single propeller usually have a rudder frame which is part of the hull and to which the propeller tube and rudder are fitted. Sometimes it also contains the outboard bearing. Ships with more than one propeller, mostly large warships, have outriggers to give extra support to the shafts which extend far beyond the hull. These outriggers then contain the outboard bearings. They are of wood or metal, depending on the diameter of the propeller shaft tube, and one side is fitted to the hull, the other to the tube. One can use epoxy cement which allows a smooth flowing form to be

5.4.   Propeller shaft with propeller.

5.5. Propeller frame
with propeller and
rudder (Moorcock).

5.6. Position of propeller shafts,
outriggers, propellers and rudders.
The parts should be regularly
lubricated with grease or oil.

obtained. If the outriggers are of wood they can be sanded to shape. Sometimes the strengthening member is of the form shown in Fig. 5.7 which can be of thin wood or metal. Once again, use epoxy cement. Where the hull is thick or where there are external supports the hole must be so drilled that the motor shaft and the propeller shaft are in line. This is not always easy unless the motor is (temporarily) fitted.

For this reason the subject will be dealt with at some length here although propulsion is dealt with in the following chapter. It is in this stage of hull construction that propeller shafts and rudder can (and sometimes must) be fitted. The description goes for wooden as well as plastic hulls.

Installing the motor

The motor supports form part of the hull. They are temporarily glued in place, mark well, temporarily. Put the hardwood supports in place, with the motor just resting on top, so that the motor shaft is more or less in line with the opening through which the propeller shaft tube will pass. Pack the spaces under the supports with wedge shaped pieces of waste material or with blocks and laths, which can then be glued in place.

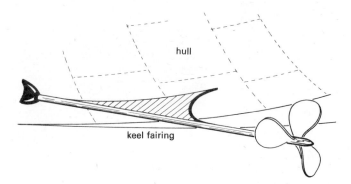
hull

keel fairing

5.7.   Outrigger connects portside propeller shaft tube to the hull.

Check if the motor is in line by fitting a coupling on the shaft and, after sliding the propeller shaft and tube through the hole from the outside, fit this also to the coupling. Adjust the tube in the (oversized) hole until motor and shaft are in line. Motor and shaft should not be more than 5° from the horizontal. See Fig. 5.8. Once the propeller shaft is in the right position use small wedges to clamp the tube in position. Fix in position with a little glue and check again the position of motor support, motor and propeller shaft.

As a final check one can connect the motor to a battery with an ammeter in series. Let the motor run and adjust it on its supports until the meter shows the lowest possible reading. With everything lined-up glue all the wedges in their final position (without moving them). Let everything thoroughly harden and make a final check.

If the meter still shows the same reading disconnect the motor from the coupling and remove it. The propeller shaft and tube can be left in place. If necessary the motor support can be further strengthened by pouring cement round. When this has hardened the motor support and hull will become an inseparable whole. Pour glue round the propeller shaft housing supporting it as necessary with blocks or wedges.

Some synthetic resin cements tend to attack plastic hulls and epoxy resins generate heat as they harden and can cause a hull to warp. It is best to add the cement a little at a time. With polyvynil acetate wood glues one has no trouble but they do take a time to harden when used in quantity.

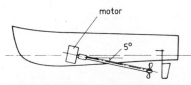

5.8. Motor and propeller shaft in line.

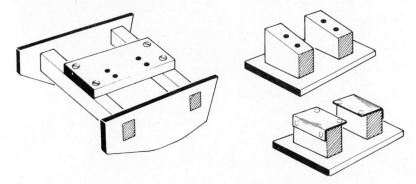

5.9.   Some examples of motor supports.

Later one can make the electric motor fast with woodscrews or with nuts and bolts if the underside is still accessible. It depends on the model drawing and the construction. Care should be taken that the propeller shaft doesn't get damaged while finishing off the ship. Models with multiple motors and propeller shafts can be dealt with in the same way as the above unless the construction drawing says otherwise.

Internal combustion engine

Those who are building a racing boat instead of a scale model may use an internal combustion engine, those for boats usually being water-cooled.

Engines must be so installed that they do not tear themselves out of the boat when starting. Motor blocks usually form a whole with the hull, the motor being fastened to it via a metal plate that is anchored with bolts, nuts and locknuts. Rubber supports are needed for motor, coupling and exhaust in order to dampen vibration and noise. The effects of vibration should not be underestimated, neither should the effects of

5.10. High requirements are set on the installation of internal combustion engine, propeller shaft and propeller shaft tube (HMBC racing team, NL).

fuel on the structure. Apart from high requirements being essential for the motor support the same is true for that of the propeller shaft.

Permanent lubrication of the shaft and a proper mounting are no luxury if one remembers that flat out such a motor can

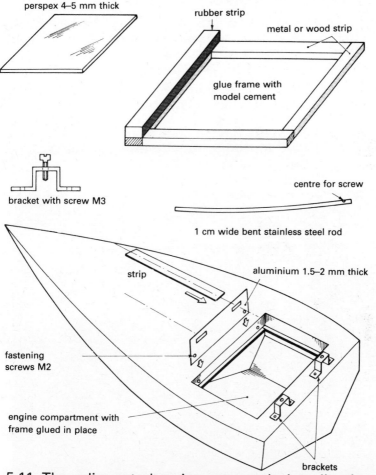

perspex 4–5 mm thick

rubber strip

metal or wood strip

glue frame with
model cement

bracket with screw M3

centre for screw

1 cm wide bent stainless steel rod

strip

aluminium 1.5–2 mm thick

fastening
screws M2

engine compartment with
frame glued in place

brackets

5.11. The radio control equipment must be in a vibration absorbing watertight compartment. Two stainless steel strips are pushed through the slots and the brackets to clamp the hatch (which is fitted with rubber strips) in place. (C. Leppers, NL).

reach 20,000 r.p.m. The motor must be so mounted that it can easily be removed for maintenance. One can buy special parts for the propeller shafts and rudders of racing models. The coupling is usually more massive and differs somewhat from those used for scale models. Finally the radio control must be fitted in a watertight compartment and be vibration free, something that requires some experience.

Racing such a boat is also an experience in itself. They can reach 65 km/hr (40 m.p.h.) and one really must learn to 'drive'. A beginner will have his work cut out not to smash the boat into the bank within the first couple of minutes.

Racing boats can also be powered by electric motors. These are the large powerful sort used for model planes. They draw so much current that the battery is rapidly exhausted. Some are water-cooled, some have a cooling fin mounted on the drive shaft. Instead of lead acid batteries or dry cells use is

5.12.   A sturdy stand is no luxury for this heavy model of the Yeh Hung (Orient Overseas Lines) built by Kosta Angelow from Bulgaria.

made of rechargeable nickel-cadmium or silver-zinc batteries which can withstand a high current drain without damage.

The hull has now reached the point that one can start thinking about the superstructure, but first we must build a stand. On a base plate that is half to three-quarters the length of the ship and a couple of centimetres broader, support brackets having the profile of the hull are screwed and glued. If necessary sand to shape and cover the bearing surfaces with foam rubber, foam plastic, draught strip, or felt, so as to avoid damage to the hull. If the hull fits properly in its stand it won't shift or fall over during transport.

We have paid a lot of attention to hull construction but no more than is necessary when one thinks that a ship depends wholly on the hull: even the decks fit better. Although it is not to be advised one can fiddle a bit with the superstructure, but not with the hull. A well built hull will sail better than a poor one, and the experience one has gained will be put to good use on the superstructure. But before proceeding to that we will use the following chapter to deal with propulsion and steering in some detail.

6 Propulsion and steering

Most model ships will be propelled in the usual way, that is to say, with a propeller. With ships of the last century one may encounter a paddle steamer which we will deal with in Chapter 9. The same goes for sailing.

It is important that the power of the motor is most efficiently used. Not only the motor is important but also the surface area, diameter and pitch of the propeller. It is also worth while examining the term power in more detail. The motor uses electricity as fuel, which has to be stored in the model, either in accumulators or in batteries, or liquid fuel or gas in internal combustion engines and steam engines.

There are a number of points which are closely related to propulsion and in this chapter we will try to throw sufficient light on all these subjects.

The invention and rapidly growing use of the steam engine confronted shipbuilders with the problem of attaining maximum speed for the lowest engine weight and the minimum fuel consumption. The water resistance of models was measured in towing tanks and by adapting the shape of the hull attempts were made to reduce resistance. Initially ships were driven by paddles which eventually gave way to screws, a form of propulsion originally discovered by Archimedes. The properties of this new 'propeller' were intensively studied by the use of models. As a result one gained the modern ideas of streamlining and also a good deal of insight into how results measured on models could be converted into usable data for full scale ships and their propulsion units.

Merger partners

In principle shipbuilders deal with three units that can be compared to three partners in a merger. Each partner has his own characterisitics and the three must be so combined that they work well together.

82

Partner number 1 is the hull. He resists movement (water resistance), and the faster one tries to move him the more he resists.

Partner number 2 is the propulsion unit which has to overcome the resistance of the hull. He does nothing for nothing, he demands energy in the form of electricity or liquid fuel. He is, furthermore, somewhat choosy about the conditions in which he works, especially with regard to r.p.m. One can easily get him to work at a less favourable speed which leads to either high fuel consumption or a low energy transfer, to the final partner, the screw. At the same time the life of the motor is also endangered.

As partner number 3 the task of the screw is to convert the energy given to him into propulsion power. The screw is the most difficult of the partners. The faster the ship goes the less propulsion power he generates and that is just when the hull offers the most resistance. And as the final difficulty, the screw usually requires a totally different speed to that at which the motor operates most efficiently.

The fourth partner, the reduction unit

The gear box, or reduction unit, enters the scene as a sort of broker between partners 2 & 3. His function is to adapt the engine and screw to each other so that both can work at maximum efficiency. The small amount of energy that the gearbox needs (converted to heat), is amply rewarded by the greater efficiency that one gains. The task of the model builder is to find the right combination of screw, gearbox and motor for his ship.

Propeller perils

One can't take any old motor and connect it with a propeller shaft (with or without gearbox) to the screw. At least not if one wants to come close to the scale speed with the use of the least energy (which means longer sailing). One needs to go about it another way. What diameter propeller and with what pitch? And apropos of pitch, what is pitch, actually?

Pitch is the distance a screw would travel for one turn if no slip occurred. Pitch ratio is the ratio between screw diameter and pitch. If the diameter of a screw is 50 mm, for example, and the pitch is also 50 mm, then the pitch ratio is 50:50 or 1:1. If the diameter were 100 mm in the above example, then the ratio would be 100:50 or 2:1. Apart from pitch and diameter we have also mentioned slip. This is the difference between the theoretical advance made by the screw in each revolution and the actual advance made.

One can make this clearer by considering an ordinary bolt, if it is turned in a nut. With each turn it advances a specific distance depending on the pitch of the thread. If one turns the same bolt in a soft material such as clay, it just turns without advancing, it slips. A too heavily loaded ship will cause considerable propeller slip; it won't progress.

Put simply, the screws in Fig. 6.1. have different pitches. Among other things the pitch of a screw depends on the angle it makes with the hub to which it is fixed. The greater the angle, the greater the pitch. The greater the pitch the higher the power required of the motor, in fact the greater the pitch the more water must be pushed through the blades, which is why one often hears that an electric motor has burnt out, simply because either the pitch or the diameter of the screw was too great. In such cases, more power is demanded of the motor than it can deliver, with the inevitable result.

In the reverse case, when the pitch is too small, a motor can easily race away; in other words it turns to little effect and the ship progresses with difficulty.

From the foregoing it will be clear that for optimal efficiency pitch and r.p.m. must be adapted to each other, which means that an alteration in r.p.m. means an alteration in pitch.

6.1. Schematic representation of a screw with small pitch (left) and large pitch (right).

Clockwise and anti-clockwise screws

Screws can be either clockwise or anti-clockwise. Clockwise means turning in a clockwise direction when viewed from aft and with the ship moving forward. The blades are set as in Fig. 5.5. A screw that turns clockwise will tend to push the stern to starboard.

If it is reversed the ship will go astern and the stern will be pushed to port. This sidewards thrust can be something of a problem, but it can also be put to good use (see Chapter 12). It will be clear that screws that turn anti-clockwise behave in the opposite way. One can meet clockwise and anti-clockwise screws on double (and multiple) propeller ships. At the same r.p.m., the two screws (which rotate in opposite directions) equalise each other. This can be quite an advantage when manoeuvring, especially if the screws can be separately controlled.

To recapitulate:

1. A screw that turns clockwise will, when going ahead, force the stern to starboard and the bow to port (Fig. 6.2 A).
2. A screw that turns clockwise will, when going astern, force the stern to port and the bow to starboard. (Fig. 6.2 B).
3. An anti-clockwise screw will, when going ahead, force the stern to port and the bow to starboard. (Fig. 6.2 C).

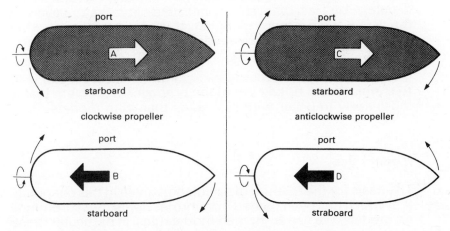

6.2.   The influence of propeller rotation on steerage.

4. An anti-clockwise screw will, when going astern, force the stern to starboard and the bow to port. (Fig. 6.2 D).

Cavitation

With the use of motors which impart a high speed to the propeller shaft, it can happen that the choice of the wrong screw can lead to the phenomenon known as cavitation.

When a screw turns a pressure is created on one side and a 'vacuum' on the other. The screw thrusts on one side and draws on the other. In general the motion imparted to the ship depends for 60% on the vacuum and for the rest on the pressure. Water boils at a specific temperature. At water level and with a pressure of one atmosphere water boils at 100 °C. At great heights where the pressure is lower water may boil at 60°C. With a pressure of 0.02 atmosphere water will boil at a temperature of 20°C! This last temperature is that which we find in general in the summer months in our ponds and lakes. Should the vacuum at the screw reach 0.02 atmosphere, then the adjacent water will boil and the water will become steam. The efficiency of the screw will thereby be greatly impaired because instead of water flowing over it we now have steam bubbles which disturb the working profile.

This boiling is known as cavitation. The steam bubbles that develop don't last long, simply because a little way away from the screw the pressure is higher. It is obvious, though, that this 'racing' of the screw leads to a loss of efficiency and speed.

If cavitation should occur in exceptional measure it can lead to chunks being ripped out of the propeller, a problem that is more likely to occur with real ships than with models.

Model rules

The basis for the method of calculation given in this chapter is that which has been gained from professional measurements on models. We use so-named model rules, in particular those relating to ships and ships' propellers.

6.3　During a trial run the Bismarck of T. Hammer (GB) used 13.6 A at 6 V. The three Decaperm motors are coupled direct to the screws.

Model rules are formulas that relate the linear relationship of two identically shaped objects to the actual working situation, such as the speed or r.p.m. of the objects.

Account is also taken of the medium (water) in which the objects exist. In this way we can have 'scale speed', 'scale r.p.m.' and 'scale power'. If only we had 'scale water' there wouldn't be any problem, that is a water with a viscosity in scale with the model. However, the model sails in the same sort of water as the real ship, which is the reason why we have scale effects, whereby fundamentally simple scale rules often work out in practice as far from simple.

Thanks to intensive model study one now has a good method of calculation that virtually eliminates scale effects.

On the basis of measurements and screw characteristics a shipbuilder can find the eventual way to a definite hull shape and can determine what engines must be installed to deliver the necessary power. Furthermore, he then knows precisely which propeller is needed and what the revolutions must be to achieve the desired propulsion.

On the basis of these 'genuine' facts a model builder can follow the same path to determine the power, the screw, and r.p.m. needed for his model. The calculations are simple and a small electronic calculator can simplify them even further.

6.4.	To obtain the same scale values one must base one's calculations on the original ship. (Deutsches Bundesarchiv).

Information about the original

What can one achieve with the calculation and how does one come by the necessary facts? Well, in most cases the model is derived from a real ship and it is the information about this we must try to get hold of. Sometimes this information is supplied with the kit, either on the instruction drawing or in the building instructions. Otherwise one must turn to the line operating the ship or to the yard where it was built. Should all these doors be closed one can use a similar ship as example or make a compromise. A similar ship can, of course, always be found. Fishing boats of the same class vary little in speed, and this is true for very nearly every kind of ship. Naturally this sort of thing is a last resort, because one can hardly speak of 'scale' in such circumstances.

Characteristics

From the information one has one can derive the following:

From the power and speed of the original, one can determine

88

the power that must be delivered to the propeller of the model. One can then determine the pitch and diameter of the screw and the r.p.m. at which it must operate. From the characteristics of available electric motors one can determine which can deliver that power, increased, of course, with the losses that can be expected in reduction gear and propeller shaft.

Naturally, the efficiency of the motor must be as high as possible. From the speeds of motor and screw one can determine the reduction ratio needed. The speed of the motor is fixed for a given voltage and current.

Only now can the private wishes of the model builder be taken into account:

- he doesn't want to use a gear box and wants to use a particular brand of screw (Graupner, Robbe, Ripmax, etc.). In general he will have to be content with a smaller screw than the scale demands.
- he is willing to accept a gearbox on the condition that the screw is more or less to scale.
- he is determined that the screw be to scale.

Note: In the first case the screw will be barely effective which leads inevitably to poor efficiency. In the second case the pitch of the 'scale' screw is fixed. This will automatically fix the reduction ratio and the r.p.m. In general, these will deviate from standard values so that some sort of compromise has to be made.

If one has the courage, knowledge and skill to make a propeller oneself, one can make it with diameter, shape, pitch and the number of blades completely to scale. If necessary the pitch can be adapted so that one can use a standard reduction gear, and thus with the most advantageous efficiency.

A novice model builder will feel little obligation to perform a series of 'difficult' calculations before the propulsion unit is installed. Any propulsion unit is good enough provided the model sails – and as soon as possible! The chance of disappointment is fairly large in this case. The more careful model builder will try to achieve greater perfection. The most important things for him are scale speed and low energy consumption.

6.5 A Monoperm Super Special electric motor.

6.6. The Monoperm motor coupled to a 'pile' reduction gear (a). The planetary gears comprise separate parts so that one can assemble any desired reduction ratio.

6.7. A Hectoperm motor with a 1:2 reduction.

Practical motors

So now we come to the question as to which motors are suitable as propulsion units. In fact there are only a few permanent magnet d.c. motors that are suitable. The German Marx-Lüder range, for example, which includes the well-known Monoperm, Monoperm super, the Decaperm and the Hectoperm. Taycol and Mabuchi motors are also often used. They are good motors but they have the disadvantage that there are no suitable gearboxes for them.

Sometimes one finds someone using an old windscreen wiper motor or a motor from an electric heater. These motors are certainly powerful but they consume an awful lot of current and it is impossible to fit a standard gearbox to them. Above all they are too large to install.

Metal gears are often used in gearboxes; they are encased but can be rather noisy. They can also cause interference with the radio control. Synthetic gears are best if one must build the gearbox oneself.

Marx motors have the advantage that suitable gearboxes (planetary) can be obtained and that the characteristics of the motors are published. With normal use they have a life of 1,000 working hours. The case may run at a maximum temperature of 90°C. All motors of the series can be had in both 6 V and 12 V versions. Under certain circumstances one can also use them with a higher voltage (over voltage) but one must be careful with respect to the current. The product of the voltage and current (power in watts) shown on the motor must never be exceeded because this will reduce the life of the motor.

For example, the maximum current for a Decaperm is specified as 7 A at 6 V. The product is 42 watts which must not be exceeded even with over voltage. Should we run it at 9 V the maximum allowable current would be 42/9 = 4.6 A. This value can be more easily exceeded under slight overload conditions than with the normal voltage. The only advantage of over voltage is the higher revs and a better efficiency; the revs must in any case be reduced.

Practically all of the Marx-Lüder motors can be fitted with specially made reduction gearboxes. They are of synthetic material and the required reduction can be obtained by self assembled parts. Reductions of between 1:3 and 1:43 200 can be made.

The motors and gearboxes can be used for a variety of purposes and the required combination can be assembled for a wide variety of ships. The motor should be connected to the supply via a fuse (see Chapter 7). Information about motors is collated at the end of this book.

The characteristics of the Marx-Lüder motors are published (based on average factory values). For other motors one must turn to the manufacturer or importer, or measure the values oneself. Small motors that are unsuitable for propulsion can still perform useful service in driving radar antennae, fans, anchor winches and suchlike. But remember to suppress radio interference by means of chokes and capacitors.

Calculating propulsion

The subject so often mentioned in this chapter, scale propulsion, will now be dealt with. The solution will not always be perfect, but the calculations will lead to a reasonable choice of propulsion system.

6.8. This model of the U.S. Coast and Geodetic Survey vessel (here seen during construction) is used as example for the 'van den Bussche recipe' (see also Fig. 4.19).

On the face of it the calculations seem complicated, but if one follows the instructions carefully, one only has to fill in a single equation and use the data so obtained to derive the required values from the curves and diagrams that will be found at the back of this book. To assist in following the method a calculation is given for one of the author's models:

the M.S. Wesselina, of the U.S. Coast Guard, the basic data of which will be found (in italics) in the equations and curves.

This totally new procedure was developed from existing equations by the Chairman of the Hague Model Boat Club, Ir. H.K.J. van den Bussche.

Known as The van den Bussche method in Holland, this approach was an important step towards better sailing characteristics and greater efficiency. It is best to make a tracing of the curves and set out the lines for one's own calculation on the tracing.

Determining screw, motor and reduction

Standard approach No. 1 which should be rigorously followed.

Name: Wesselina   Scale 1 : 24

Required data (original):
Installed power per screw (N_o) HP $N_o = 600\,HP$
Top speed (V_o) m/s (1 knot = 0.5 m/s) $V_o = 10\,m/s$
Screw diameter (D_o) metres $D_o = 0.9\,m$
Number of blades (u) $u = 3$
Number of screws (v) $v = 2$

Non-essential but informative information

Screw pitch (H) metres $H = m$
Screw revs (n_o) r.p.m. $n_o = r.p.m.$

Calculation method (model)

1. Model scale: 1 α $\alpha = 24$
2. Propeller shaft diameter (d) $d = 4\,mm$
2a. Scale speed

$$V_s = \frac{1}{\sqrt{\alpha}}\ V_o \rightarrow V_s = \frac{1}{\sqrt{24}}\ x\ 10 \rightarrow V_s = 2.04\,m/s$$

For the square root see page 243

3. Scale power per screw

$$N_s = 1\,000 \times \frac{N_o\,(HP)}{\alpha\,3\frac{1}{2}}\ W \longrightarrow \frac{1\,000 \times 600}{24^{3\frac{1}{2}}} \longrightarrow N_s = 8.86\,W$$

$(\alpha^{3\frac{1}{2}} = \alpha \times \alpha \times \alpha \times \alpha \times \alpha$ or $V\alpha^7$

4. Effective speed: (sailing speed diminished by . . . . current)
$V_e = 0.8\,V_s$ (single screw)
$V_e = 0.9\,V_s$ (twin screw) $\longrightarrow$ $V_e = 1.84$ m/s
$V_e = 0.84\,V_e$ (triple screw)

5. Screw diameter:

$$D_s = \frac{1\,000\,D_o}{\alpha} \quad\longrightarrow\quad D_s = \frac{1\,000 \times 0.9}{24} \quad\longrightarrow\quad D_s = 37.5\,\text{mm}$$

6. Propulsion factor

$$Z = \sqrt[5]{\frac{D^2_s \times V^3_e}{N_s}} = \quad\longrightarrow\quad \sqrt[5]{\frac{37.5^2 \times 1.84^3}{8.86}} \quad\longrightarrow\quad Z = 3.97\,\text{mm}$$

7. Ideal pitch and sailing conditions:
From curve 1 one can determine:
Pitch ratio H/D $H/D = 0.77$
Propulsion coefficient λ (lamda) $\lambda = 0.52$
Screw efficiency η_i (eta) $\eta_i = 0.6$

8. Screw revolutions:

$$n_s = \frac{60\,000 \times V_e}{\lambda \times D_s} \quad\longrightarrow\quad \frac{60\,000 \times 1.84}{0.52 \times 38} \quad\longrightarrow\quad n_s = 5587\,\text{r.p.m.}$$

9. Losses in propeller shaft (diameter: d mm)
$N_a = n_s \times d \times 10^4 \longrightarrow$ $5587 \times 4 \times 10^4 \longrightarrow$ $N_a = 2.24\text{W}$

10. Required motor power per screw:

$N_m = N_s \times N_a \longrightarrow$ $8.86 + 2.24 \longrightarrow$ $N_m = 11.1$ W

Note: Figures that are not in italics are fixed values that are valid for all scale calculations!

Having worked through the equations from point 1 to point 6 one consults curve No. 1 Appendix 2. (page 245), see also point 7.

The pitch ratio (H/D) one obtains from the curve will usually differ from the pitch ratios obtainable. Should one decide to use an available screw that has a diameter that differs little from the scale diameter, then the propulsion factor should be calculated anew using point 6.

Depending on whether the screw has three or four blades one uses curve IIa or IIb, respectively. Here one will find curves for specific pitch ratios and (less steep) curves for specific Z values. Having found the point at which the H/D line cuts the Z line one can read off the coefficient of propulsion (λ) on the horizontal axis. The dashed lines enable one to estimate the screw efficiency (η).

If one uses screws supplied by Graupner (the most commonly available screw) one has the choice of three-bladed screws with a pitch ratio H/D of 0.5 or two-bladed screws with a pitch ratio of 0.75. With the two-bladed types one can also obtain double pitch screws with a pitch ratio of 1.5. Only in the three-bladed range can one obtain clockwise and anti-clockwise screws. To facilitate the calculations curve IV has been derived from curve IIa specifically for screws with a pitch ratio of 0.5, 0.75, and 1.5.

The efficiency so found will normally differ from that of the scale propeller and, therefore, the power needed to drive it (calculated in point 3) will need to be adapted. If the calculated value was η_i and the value for the screw is η, then the requisite power can be corrected by:

$$* N'_s = \frac{\eta'_i}{\eta} \; N_s \text{ watts}$$

Should N'_s differ significantly from N_s then it is worth recalculating Z using N'_s. With the new value of Z one can return to curve IIa (or IIb or IV, as the case may be) to recalculate values for λ and η. The final value of η is used to correct the screw power. Beginning with point 8 one can now proceed further with the calculation and thus derive:

1. The requisite motor power per screw, in watts.
2. The screw revolutions, in r.p.m.
3. The scale speed, in m/s.

*Corrected values are indicated by an accent, thus N'.

The information thus gained enables one to choose a motor and reduction ratio. For multi-propeller ships one must also decide whether one motor can drive all the propellers or whether each propeller needs a separate motor.

In the foregoing a number of factors have been mentioned which make Marx motors attractive. For example, virtually every motor in the range can be supplied with a planetary gearbox with which virtually any reduction ratio can be obtained. Furthermore, the motors are efficient and their characteristics are defined. Because the characteristics of other makes of motor are unpublished, we will have to ignore them, which must not be interpreted as saying that they are less good.

For models in Class F2 (scale model class, see Chapter 12), the following motors of the Marx range are of interest:

Monoperm –	TM
Monoperm super –	TMS
Decaperm –	TD
Hectoperm –	TH

Depending on what we have calculated as the required power, the choice is determined as follows:

TM or TMS if the required power N_m is between 10 W and 20 W, or to put it another way: 20 W N_m 10W.

TM(S)	if	20 W $> N_m > 10$ W
TD or TH	if	45 W $> N_m > 20$ W
TH	if	75 W $> N_m > 45$ W.

In choosing the motor the following points need to be considered.

In respect of efficiency the TMS is to be preferred to the TM

6.9. The 32 kg Moorcock uses 3.2 A at a top (scale) speed of 4.8 km/hr. The 108 mm propeller is driven by a 6 V Hectoperm motor connected to a 12 V battery. A reduction of 1:9 is used.

if the power required is less than 10 W. That the TM is shorter may also be decisive in choosing it.

Above 15 W the TH has a higher efficiency than the TD, which can be used up to 45 W. Here, too, the length and the price may lead to the TD being chosen. Another point is that the speed of the TD is higher, which in conjunction with a standard reduction may lead to a better matching between motor speed and screw speed.

For the usual supply voltages (up to 12 V) only the 6 V types are used. As we have seen, the limitation is not so much the voltage as the current. If the model builder wants a higher speed than the scale speed then this will affect the motor chosen and the yet to be determined reduction ratio. Diagrams IIIa, IIIb, IIIc and IIId have been drawn in order to assist in arriving at concrete values. They are for the motor types TM, TMS, TD and TH, respectively.

These diagrams (actually they are nomograms) are divided into four fields.

Left of the origin on the horizontal axis one can read off the motor power required, N_m (in w) and the screw speed in r.p.m. (n_s). These values relate to the scale speed.

If one wants a higher speed than the scale speed one draws a vertical line from N_m up to where it cuts the ø line. From this point one draws a line horizontally to the right to cut the vertical axis from which one can read off the requisite motor power ($ø^3.N_m$). In order to find the overspeed one draws, in the same way, a vertical line downward from the n_s value to the ø line and then horizontally across to the lower vertical axis. Here one can read off the screw speed ($ø.n_s$). The lines (R) in the right-hand lower field are the reduction ratios. Draw a horizontal line to the right from the screw speed to where it cuts a specific reduction ratio line and, vertically above this point one can read off the motor speed (r.p.m.) on the horizontal axis.

The right-hand upper field shows the motor characteristics which relate speed ($ø^3.N_m$) to speed ($ø.R.n_s$) and supply voltage. *In this characteristic curve account is taken of a 1 V voltage drop in the controller and supply lines. In other words the voltage on the motor brushes is 1 V less than the supply voltage.* This diagram also shows the current drain and the efficiency of the motor.

Using the diagram

We used earlier the example of the M.S. Wesselina and derived under point 8 of the formula $N_m = 11.1$ W and $n_s = 5,587$ rpm. In this case each screw has a separate motor for which we choose a TMS motor (diagram IIIa). To sail at scale speed (ø = 1), assuming a power supply of 12 V, (to use 6 V one should alter the drawn-in line in the example) we find that the reduction needed will be 2.5. Unfortunately, this is not a standard reduction, the lowest obtainable is 1:3. For this reason we must alter the pitch of the screw (pitch and revolutions are mutually interdependent) in the ratio of 3:2.5.

The pitch ratio can be found in the formula under point 7: H/D = 0.77. The corrected pitch ratio will now be:

$$H/D = \frac{3}{2.5} \times 0.77 = 0.924$$

The blade angle β at 75% of the diameter of the blade can be found using the formula:

$$\text{The tangent of } \beta \ (\tan \beta) = \frac{H/D}{0.75 \times \pi} = \frac{0.924}{0.75 \times \pi} = 0.39216$$

(see also the drawing in Appendix 2, page . . .)

This value can be looked up in the table and the angle found to be 21°25′, which means that $\beta_{0.75} = 21°25′$. At 75% of the screw diameter, the blade forms an angle of 21°25′ with the hub. The

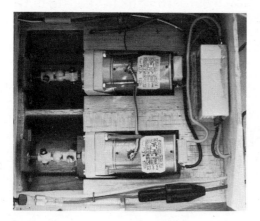

6.10. Two Monoperm Super Special electric motors with a reduction of 1:3. They are connected to a 12 V battery and together consume 2.8 A (M.S. Wesselina).

working point of the motor on the 12 V line lies at a current drain of 1.4 A and an efficiency that is very nearly optimum at 72%!

This 1:3 reduction and the greater pitch have changed the picture somewhat. The easily obtainable Robbe screw with a diameter of 40 mm and a pitch ratio H/D = 0.9 is likely to form a good combination with the 1:3 reduction ratio.

If no reduction is used, R = 1, therefore, one can see from the diagram (dashed line) that the requisite power and revolutions are delivered with approx. 8 V working voltage and a current drain of 3 A. 3 A happens to be the maximum current for the motor, no reserve will be built in, therefore. Apart from the motor working continuously at peak capacity the efficiency has dropped to 52%. At a voltage higher than 8 V the motor will burn out!

To illustrate the effect of speed reduction we will assume that an ideal motor can be had. If one now makes the requirement that the speed shall be 15% higher than the scale speed, ø = 1.15, the chain dotted line shows the new working point of the motor and the reduction required: more or less 1:2. Changing the reduction from 1:2.5 to 1:2 (bearing in mind the ideal screw) means that the motor must deliver 16.8 W in place of 11.1 W. The current drain rises to about 2.2 A and the efficiency drops to just under 70%, which is still very good.

If we would now like to know what the result would be of choosing a TM motor in place of a TMS, we only need to draw the same lines in diagram IIIa. We will see that in order to sail at scale speed (ø = 1) a reduction of 1:2.3 is required with an ideal screw. From the working point of the motor one can see that the current drain will be 1.9 A, 0.5 A higher than with the TMS. The efficiency is proportionately lower being only 52%.

If we finally want to know what the relationships are if we use an existing three-blade screw from the Robbe range with a diameter D = 40 mm and H/D = 0,9 then we calculate (point 6 in the formula):

$$Z = \sqrt[5]{\frac{40^2 \times 1.84^3 = 4.08}{8.86}}$$

In diagram IIa one looks for the intersection of the Z = 4.08 line with that of H/D = 0.9. The line Z = 4.08 must be interpolated between the lines Z = 4 and Z = 4.25 in the ratio 8:17. There being 17 'distance units' between 4.08 and 4.25. The intersection of these lines corresponds with a λ of 0.58 and an efficiency η of 0.61. The efficiency is even higher than with the ideal screw, which is not surprising if one thinks that larger diameter and greater pitch combine to give a higher efficiency. According to point 8 of the formula the revolutions for this screw:

$$n_s = \frac{60\,000 \times 1.84}{0.58 \times 40} = 4\,760 \text{ rpm.}$$

In diagram IIIb (ø = 1) this speed intersects with a reduction of 1:3. The Robbe screw, a standard reduction of 1:3 and the 6 V TMS motor apparently harmonise completely for this ship.

6.11.   This 150 cm long model has two propeller shafts driven direct by Decaperm motors. The current consumption is over 10 A. The propeller used is not ideal (M.S.V. Schwelm, BRD).

Propulsion without reduction

In the foregoing one has seen how one can determine the most favourable pitch for a screw of scale diameter. One could also see that with a given type of motor and supply voltage a reduction is required that is usually unobtainable with standard parts. A little adaptation of the pitch in order to use a standard gearbox leads to little loss of efficiency.

Further, that when the diameter and pitch of an available type of screw are not fully in accordance with a scale screw, one can still determine the most favourable reduction. Finally we have learned that a scale screw can be driven direct at a lower voltage and can deliver scale speed, albeit at the cost of a very low efficiency and a motor that might burst into flames at any moment!

The question now remains as to whether one can use the available diagrams (for the sake of cost and simplicity) to select a standard screw which when directly driven (R = 1) can work economically. The procedure to be used is more or less identical with that used to find the most suitable reduction for a known screw.

Standard screw

All that we know about the screw we are looking for is that its diameter will probably be less than the scale diameter and that because it will be directly driven, both motor and screw will rotate at the same speed. Points 1 to 7 of the formula are calculated which gives one the ideal efficiency. One then calculates the propulsion coefficient, Z, for a number of screw diameters (less than the scale diameter). If one limits oneself to screws of the Graupner series one can use diagram IV to calculate λ and η.

The value for η will be definitely lower than the efficiency of the scale screw (point 7). The power is therefore proportionately corrected:

$$ {}^{*}N'_s = \frac{\eta_i}{\eta} \ N_s $$

*Corrected values are indicated by an accent, N'_s, for example.

101

From the corrected value Z can be redetermined, and, again using curve IV, λ and η can be determined. Should this value of η differ markedly from the value originally determined, the power should be calculated again and a new value for Z determined. Yet again curve IV is used to fix the values of λ and η.

Sticking to the example of the Wesselina, one has the choice of 20, 25, and 30 mm screws out of the Graupner three-blade series. Strangely enough, the Graupner series rises in steps of 5 mm * from 20 mm to 65 mm, but without a 35 mm. Because 20 and 25 mm look rather small we can confine ourselves to the 30 mm screw. Should that turn out to be too much for the TMS motor one can always revert to a smaller screw.

One finds now the value of Z:

$$Z = \sqrt[5]{\frac{30^2 \times 1.84^3}{8.86}} = 3.63$$

From diagram IV (H/D = 0.5) one sees that $\eta = 0.515$ and $\lambda = 0.33$. For the scale screw this was $\eta_i = 0.6$ so that, correcting:

$$N'_s = \frac{0.6}{0.515} \times 8.86 = 10.30 \, W$$

and,

$$Z' = 3.63 \sqrt[5]{\frac{0.515}{0.6}} = 3.52$$

For this last value of Z', $\eta' = 0.5$ and $\lambda' = 0.32$.

Correcting yet again:

$$N_s'' = \frac{0.6}{0.5} \times 8.86 = 10.63$$

And from curve IV: $\eta'' = 0.495$ and $\lambda'' = 0.318$.

*Now available in increments of 2.5 mm.

Because these values differ but little from those first determined (N'_s and Z') one can proceed further with the formula at point 8. The screw revolutions are then:

$$n_s = \frac{60\,000 \times 1.84}{0.318 \times 30} = 11\,570\,\text{rpm (!)}$$

At such high revolutions the shaft losses will be greater; this can be calculated using point 9 of the formula:
$N_a \times 11\,570 \times 4 \times 10^{-4} = 4.63\,\text{W}$.

These losses can be halved by using a 2 mm shaft in place of a 4 mm one. A 30 mm screw has an M2 thread, and this is the screw we have in mind.

Assuming that we remain with the 4 mm shaft, the motor power per shaft will be:
$N_a = 10.63 + 4.63 = 15.26\,\text{W}$

(10.63 is taken from the last calculation for N'_s)
Using a 2 mm shaft would result in:

$$N_a = 10.63 + \frac{4.63}{2} = 13.94\,\text{W}$$

The working point of the motor in diagram IIIb ($\varnothing = 1$ and $R = 1$), shows that scale speed will be obtained at almost 11 V. To discover what can be expected at 12 V one finds the working points that correspond to $\varnothing = 1.05$, 1.1 and 1.15. These points are joined by a smooth curve. Where this line cuts the 12 V curve one can read off the related current drain and the motor efficiency. This is shown in the diagram with a full line and for the (more favourable) 2 mm shaft with a broken line. The full line cuts the 12 V line at a point where the shaft power is 18 W at 12,400 r.p.m. The current drain is 2.4A and the efficiency at 67% can be called good. The speed is about 6% higher than scale speed ($\varnothing = 1.06$), and it would make little sense to calculate for another screw. A 35 mm Graupner screw would, certainly, demand more than 12 V to attain scale speed, let alone overspeed, if required. Drawing up a balance one will see that directly driven (without reduction) the 30 mm Graupner screw will require of the batteries

$N_e = 2 \times 2.4 \times 12 = 57.6\,\text{W}$ (with a 4 mm shaft)
$N_e = 2 \times 2.25 \times 12 = 54.0\,\text{W}$ (with a 2 mm shaft),
and if a 1:3 reduction is used with, for example, a 40 mm Robbe screw:
$N_e = 2 \times 1.4 \times 12 = 33.6\,\text{W}$.

In general one can say that the directly driven screws (even when most advantageously used) require 60% more energy than an adapted, slower screw. This is the price one must pay for a 'simple and cheap' solution, by which we mean cutting out the gearbox and coupling the shaft direct to the motor. It is clear that it is well worth while properly calculating the propulsion, if necessary, with help from someone else!

6 volt or 12 volt?

The power that must be delivered to a motor is independent of the applied voltage. Power (P) is expressed in watts (W). It is the product of voltage (V) and current (I), the last in amperes (A). In other words $P = V.I$. Now there are other relationships between voltage and current of which Ohm's law is not the least important. This law states that the voltage is equal to the product of current and resistance (R). This implies that when resistance is increased while the voltage remains the same, the current will be reduced.

Taking, for an example a motor with a power of 18 W and with a brush resistance of 1/3 Ohm, and connecting it to various voltages, we will see:

At 6 V, $I = \dfrac{18}{6} = 3$ A and the voltage drop across the brushes is

$1/3 \times 3 = 1$ V.

The power loss is thus $1 \times 3 = 3$ W.

at 12 V, $I = \dfrac{18}{12} = 1.5$ A, and, because R remains the same, $V =$

$1/3 \times 1.5 = 0.5$ V, and the power loss $= 0.5 \times 1.5 = 0.75$ W; from which one can see that increasing the voltage greatly reduces the losses.

Steam engines

Although steam propulsion is not likely to be one of the first thoughts of a novice model builder it is worth making some remarks about it.

6.12.　A self-built 3-cylinder steam engine (Jameson, GB).

6.13.　10 years has been devoted to this all-metal model (Jameson, GB).

Steam propulsion has been common enough in Britain for years. Fig. 6.12 shows a self-made 3 cylinder steam engine which propels a wholly metal passenger ship (Fig. 6.13). Ship and engine, together, took the owner 10 years to build. The owner (British, of course) exhibited the model at the European Championships at Welwyn Garden City in 1975. On the Continent, too, interest is growing for steam propulsion. In fact, one can think of no more natural propulsion system for a model steamship.

Although one can build a model steam engine entirely oneself, one can take advantage of the various parts that can be bought ready-made. Parts from Stuart Turner, for example, enable one to build a steam engine with comparatively little effort. Ready-to-use 'toy' steam engines are of little use because of their lack of economy in the use of steam. One can, of course, buy complete propulsion units for model ships, which, while not being cheap, do save an awful lot of work.

Such a propulsion unit comprises a spirit burner, a boiler, two cylinders with pistons, steam valves, crankshaft and a fly-

6.14.   A self-built steam engine suitable for propelling a medium-sized model ship (C. Kerling, NL).

wheel with pulley. The unit comes ready-mounted, its parts are of bronze, apart from a few of stainless steel.

The burner is the same as other spirit lamps where the spirit burns after being vaporised. The tank usually burns for about 20 minutes and extinguishes (for lack of fuel) before the boiler has boiled dry (at least, if one has filled the boiler).

The boiler

The boiler, like the burner, is horizontal and is fastened to the base by a bronze strap. The fire tube lies horizontally in the boiler and is bent to protrude vertically above the boiler. Here the funnel is fitted.

A control valve is fitted to the boiler which regulates the flow of steam and which itself can be controlled by a servo, which allows some control of speed. The boiler is also fitted with a nipple to which a pressure gauge (bought separately) can be fitted. The safety valve is built into the filler cap on the top of the boiler.

The engine

The actual engine comprises two vertical cylinders with steam valves. With some makes, such as the British Stuart Turner and the Japanese Saito, there may be more or less cylinders with valves. Most steam engines have double-acting cylinders and the engine starts automatically when enough steam has been raised. The steam valves are driven from the two external cranks. The crankshaft, itself, runs in bronze bearings, lubricated from a single feed. The crankshaft is sometimes enclosed in a heavy bronze case. The extremes of the crankshaft are fitted with a pulley and a flywheel. At the flywheel end one can connect the propeller shaft via a coupling. A separately obtainable reversing unit allows the direction of rotation to be controlled via a servo unit.

The shaft power of the engine is about 0.25 H.P. (0.185 KW) at about 3,000 rpm. With this data one can determine the most suitable screw, using the 'van den Bussche' method.

Although the use of a steam engine has something real about it, a disadvantage is its size. It requires an area of some 400 x

80 mm with a height of not less than 130 mm. At the same time one must find room for the receiver and servos and the necessary power source(s). This means that but few boats will suit themselves to steam propulsion, which doesn't detract from the fact that a beautifully built steam boat is a joy to behold, and is unfortunately rarely to be seen. An idea, perhaps, for some readers?

Finally, the total weight is about 1,600 grammes including fuel and water. The steam pressure is almost 1.5 kg/cm². Parts and accessories are easily obtainable.

Internal combustion engines

Internal combustion engines are rarely used in scale model ships. Exceptions include the hydrofoil craft, and a tugboat is shown in Fig. 6.15 which is also driven by an internal combustion engine. Adaptation of a model and sailing with it are something of a speciality.

Some readers, however, will already be sold on model boat racing. There are petrol, diesel and glow plug motors. There is a lot to be learned about them and those who are really interested are referred to the 'professional' literature on the subject; there is enough available. We must content ourselves with a very brief treatment of the subject.

Petrol motors

Model motors stem from the thirties where they were used for model airplanes. They were two-stroke petrol motors with a genuine ignition system, which included a coil and a spark plug. A disadvantage was the weight of the batteries and of the coil or magneto.

Diesel motors

The idea of raising the compression ratio to achieve self ignition arose in Switzerland during the last war. This got rid of the heavy battery and coil. The motor had an adjustable compression ratio via a screw on the cylinder head. After the war this sort of motor gained popularity and the petrol motor virtually disappeared. Actually the term diesel motor for this type of motor is inaccurate. With a genuine diesel motor air is drawn in and is compressed to the point at which an injection of fuel leads to instantaneous combustion. With the type of

6.15. The propulsion unit of the tugboat Ionia is a two-cylinder diesel engine. A special exhaust system gives the model the genuine (scale) engine noise (H. de Haas, NL).

motor we are discussing vaporised fuel is drawn in and is compressed to the point at which it ignites. Detonator motor might be a better term, but now everyone calls it a diesel . . .

These motors have their disadvantages. The compression ratio demands a heavy construction and the speed can be difficult to regulate and, furthermore, easy starting cannot be

6.16. A petrol engine for a fast speedboat. The tappets, water-jacket and spark-plug are clearly visible (HMBC The Hague NL).

6.17. Once the engine has been started the radio control is given a final check. (Ionia).

6.18. The compression ratio of a diesel engine is adjustable.

included amongst their better points. They are fuelled by a mixture of paraffin, castor oil and ether.

The disadvantages were sufficient that a better system was sought, especially in America, which led to the following type.

The glow plug motor

This motor, which was introduced in the fifties, has a fixed, and furthermore, lower compression ratio (lighter construction) than the diesel. An incandescent spiral is introduced into the combustion chamber to ignite the gases. In starting it is electrically heated but once the motor is running the spiral is kept incandescent by the heat of combustion and the battery can be disconnected. The fuel in the combustion chamber is ignited at the end of the compression stroke.

These engines are fuelled by methanol (= methyl alcohol). The great advantage of this new motor was that the speed was easily regulated, which, combined with the great interest in radio control at that time, ensured its popularity.

The fixed glowplug used then is now replaced by a glowplug that is screwed into the cylinder head in much the same way

110

as the sparking plugs for a car. However, they are not sparking plugs; they function differently. 'Hot' plugs and 'cold' plugs are used depending on the type of engine. These engines are very sensitive to the fuel employed. The addition of nitromethane to the fuel accelerates combustion which leads to higher revolutions. In any case these engines tend to run faster than diesel engines.

The petrol motor has not, however, given up the fight. On the contrary, it is on the comeback. There is a class of boat in which petrol motors (with a standard capacity of 35 cm³) are standard equipment. Engines from motor mowers or tree saws are ideal for this. The speed is easily regulated, and thanks to advancing technology they become smaller every day.

Summarising, one can say that diesel motors are now practically forgotten, although here and there an enthusiast may build one himself, and glowplug engines can be obtained in countless makes and types, including hotted up versions.

Fuels

Two sorts of fuels can be distinguished:
Diesel fuel: a mixture of paraffin, castor oil and ether in the

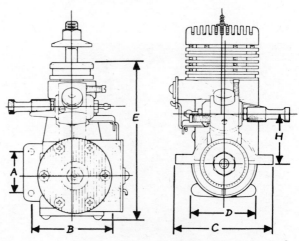

6.19. A glowplug

6.20. Front elevation and plan of a glowplug engine.

ratio 1:1:1 (this is usual, other ratios are sometimes used). Glowplug fuels: a mixture of methanol (75 to 80%), and castor oil (not normal lubrication oil which won't combine with methanol). Sometimes nitro-methane is added, to give more power. One can, of course, buy ready-to-use fuels at model shops which serve well enough but one must be sure that the fuel is suitable for one's engine.

Running in

Although the natural reaction to buying a new engine is to get sailing with it as soon as possible, one must bear in mind the running in period. Just like its larger brethren a model motor must be properly treated during its initial period of use. When you buy the motor you will receive an instruction leaflet (and a guarantee). The instruction leaflet contains, apart from a description of the motor, also instructions for running in and for the further treatment of the motor. These instructions differ so much from type to type and are so complete that we can, with all confidence commend them to you. As a novice it is wise to adhere to these instructions; failure to do so is likely to cost you the motor.

Having fitted the motor the fuel tank must be installed. The (average) fuel level in the tank should be at the same height as the carburettor (see Fig. 6.22).

6.21. Several racing boats ready for the start (HMBC racing team. NL).

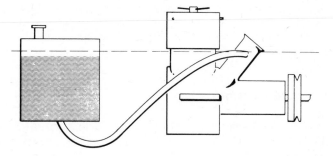

6.22. Positioning the fuel tank.

A new engine should be run on a rich mixture and as the temperature shouldn't rise too high, adequate cooling should be provided. Before actually sailing one should remember to test the radio control system.

Cooling

Most engines are air-cooled and intended for model air-planes. Engines for model boats are water-cooled and are fitted with a water jacket through which the cooling water flows. The water inlet is a small scoop fitted directly behind the propeller and connected to the water jacket via a piece of hose. The warm water from the engine is carried away by another piece of hose that connects to an outlet pipe fitted somewhat forward. See Fig.6.23. The pressure from the propeller forces water through the pipe and thereby through the system.

Noise

One can buy various sorts of exhaust and silencers for model engines. There are huge 'organ pipes' that run the full length of the boat; there are also those that are mounted inboard and which are much less striking. Without silencing, the engine produces a deafening noise which is extremely disturbing for the neighbourhood and which has led to bye-laws and such-suchlike that limit the amount of permissible noise.

In club circles noise is limited to 80 dBA (a unit associated with noise measurement), at a distance of 10 metres. Should one sail a boat individually which is usually impossible without special permission, one is advised to keep engine noise within reasonable limits.

Which engine to choose

In most kits for racing boats there is an indication of the most suitable motor, and the same is true for the screw and the propeller shaft. Rarely will one find these parts in the kit.

Power losses

In the foregoing we have given considerable attention to the motor or propulsion unit, and we cannot emphasise enough

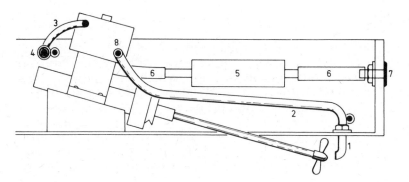

6.23. Example of a cooling system. 1 water inlet, 2 inlet hose, 3 outlet hose, 4 outlet pipe in side of hull, 5,6,7, engine exhaust system, 8 water-jacket.

the importance of the correct choice of motor and proper setting up. It is the heart of the ship but we will now leave it to delve into other matters.

Just as we strive to operate the motor at the highest efficiency (and that goes for all types of motor), so shall we logically strive to ensure that the power developed by the motor is conveyed to the screw with minimal (friction) losses. The propeller shaft wastes energy through friction losses in the bearings. Good lubrication, whether or not with the help of lubrication nipples, is essential and no more so than with internal combustion engines. Thin oil is to be preferred to grease because the last-named offers a higher resistance. Ensure therefore that the shafts run smoothly.

Couplings

In this context coupling means the coupling between motor shaft and propeller shaft. There are couplings that work the same as those in a car, but these are of a special kind. Couplings can be had in a wide range of types.

The simplest is a sort of hose that is pushed over the ends of the shafts. O.K., for a toy boat, perhaps, but not for a model.

6.24. The exhaust of this racing boat is very striking, on both sides can be seen the insulated fuel tanks (HMBC racing team, NL).

There are also spring couplings with small tubes to fit over the shafts and screws to clamp them fast. These are somewhat better.

Ball and socket couplings without a plastic insert are not to be advised because their metal to metal contact can cause interference with the radio control system, a subject that will be further dealt with in the following chapter.

The best couplings have an insulating insert or are wholly of plastic, although plastic couplings are not suitable with internal combustion engines. Cardan couplings have many advantages and can also work with a slight angle between shafts; however, the greater the angle, the higher the losses.

Cardan couplings have a cast or turned metal tube at both ends, these being screwed to suit motor and propeller shaft. These tubes are fitted with plastic claws that grip a ball joint. Between the ball joints an adjustable extension piece may be fitted. There are Cardan couplings that are made wholly from metal and which are often used with I.C. engines because of their great strength.

Before fitting the couplings it is worth filing a flat on both shafts in order to prevent the one turning without the other. At the same time the ball joint should be checked for freedom from burrs. Where necessary these should be removed with fine polishing paper (600) to ensure a smooth and flexible grip. A little light oil will ensure a low loss transmission. It is worth saying again that motor shaft, coupling and propeller shaft should be as near as possible in line. Fig. 6.26 shows a number of commonly used couplings.

6.25. A plastic Cardan shaft.

Rudder and steering system

Little thought is often given to the rudder, although it is the component that holds the ship on its course and must faithfully convert steering commands into changes of course. With radio controlled ships a servo motor is used to convert the commands received by the radio receiver into changes of rudder attitude. For the installation of a radio control system see Chapter 11.

The rudder operates in a quite simple fashion. The water from the propeller thrusts against the side of the rudder and forces the stern to one side. This causes the bow to be thrust in the opposite direction, and the entire ship turns in the desired direction. In most ships the rudder is at the stern directly behind the screw. To be as efficient as possible the rudder needs to be large enough to feel the entire thrust of the water from the propeller. This means that the rudder must reach to the deepest point of the propeller and experience has shown that the best length/breadth ratio is about 2:1, which fixes the breadth of the rudder.

It is recommended that the dimension K1 in Fig. 6.27 be larger than the mean breadth (K) and that the dimension K2 be

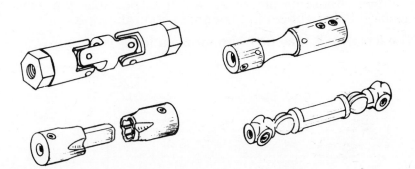

6.26.   Several types of coupling.

smaller. It is also customary to streamline the rudder as can be seen in the same drawing.

Three types of rudder are known, the blade rudder as shown in Fig. 5.5, balanced rudders as shown in Fig. 4.21 and thrusters. These last-named are a sort of jet (Fig. 6.28), that has a

117

directable function as a rudder (This is, in fact, not the case in Fig. 6.28).

The blade rudder steers most heavily because there is no self assistance. With the balanced rudder, in which part of the rudder lies before the rudder shaft, some assistance is obtained from the water acting on the fore part. The proportion of rudder before the shaft to that after is about 20:80.

The thruster functions as a jet-pipe and sometimes part of the rudder is brought within the pipe. This sort of rudder has the advantage that it also functions well when going astern. An extra advantage is the excellent protection afforded the screw. The tube should be a good fit round the propeller and the axis of the shaft should be in the plane of the screw so as to avoid the two touching when steering. With the tube in its extreme position the screw should still be wholly within the tube. This type of rudder is often used in tugs, offshore vessels, lifeboats and fishing vessels which must be manoeuvrable and often operate in shallow waters.

Rudders should be placed as far aft as possible, the exact position being shown in the construction drawing.

The distance S may be of importance for:

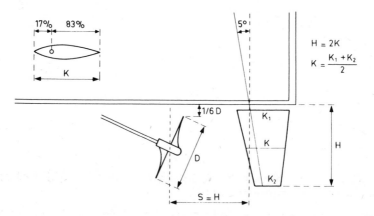

6.27. Size and position of the rudder, screw and distance between screw and rudder.

a. the installation of a cooling water inlet (internal combustion engines);

b. to give sufficient room to replace a propeller.

S should in any case not be greater than H and may even be smaller. Check the construction drawing.

When thrusters are used it is necessary to be able to dismount the rudder shaft, therefore the use of (locked) nuts is recommended. Once the shaft has been disconnected from the thruster tube it will be easy to remove the shaft.

Every ship sails more slowly when making a turn. Partly because of the resistance offered by the rudder, and partly because the ship itself offers more resistance when travelling sideways (even partially).

With double screw boats one can either fit one rudder behind each propeller or a single rudder on the centre-line. In the latter case an increase of 50% in rudder area will be required. Large scale models will (owing to their slower speed and the reduced effect of the rudder) require a larger rudder. The height of the rudder can be kept the same but its breadth should be increased to 4/5 the height. The rudder shaft should not be set at an angle of more than 5° otherwise part of the steering power will be directed downward and not aft. Furthermore the screw efficiency will be reduced.

Mounting the steering arm on the servo

The steering arm which is fitted crosswise to the rudder is connected to the servo by a rod (steering arms can be bought but they are also easy to make out of strong plastic). One end of the rod is clipped into holes in the servo disc. The holes enable one to centre the rudder and to adjust the correct distance. See also Figs. 5.1 to 5.3.

One need not use links as one can also bend the steering rod at right angles. The distances a and b, the one at the servo and the other at the steering arm should be pretty well equal. Variations here alter the throw of the rudder. If b is made smaller the throw will be increased and vice versa. The same is true at a; make a larger and the throw will be greater, make it smaller and the throw will be smaller. The installation should be such that the throw is equal both sides of centre and that it

119

does not exceed 30° to 40°. Above 40° the rudder will act more as a brake than as a better means of steering. Mounting the steering rod is not likely to give any difficulty. One should ensure that servo disc and rudder arm are at the same height, so that the steering rod is horizontal. Check with the drawing and follow any instruction in the instruction sheet.

Should the distance between servo and rudder be exceptionally great or should they not be at the same height one can also make use of Bowden cables. These are obtainable in various lengths from model shops and are used mostly to control airplane rudders. These cables are also made of plastic and are fitted with links just like steering rods. Fitting

6.28. Screw protectors (acting at the same time as jet thrusters) on the model of the tugboat Smit Pioneer. The ship has two balanced rudders.

6.29. The distance between the bottom of the ship and the blade tip of the propeller must be at least 1/6th of the diameter of the propeller.

120

instructions are usually included in the packing so that few problems should arise.

The steering servo and the rod (or cable) should be so adjusted that when the servo is in the neutral position the rudder stands perfectly fore and aft. When one turns the control on the transmitter carefully to left or right, the rudder should adopt precisely the same angle. On returning the control to the middle the rudder should return to the neutral position. (see also Chapter 11).

6.30   Servo and rudder connected together.

Servos and speed controls

The last part of this Chapter will be devoted to the use of servos and one or more speed controls. Not to the electronics used in this sort of equipment but in the use of the equipment itself. For those who wish to know more about the electronics there is literature available.

A radio control may comprise one or more servos or speed controls. What is a servo? It is an electric motor with a reduction gear which is used to drive the steering arm. An electronic circuit built into the receiver and servo ensures that the servo makes the same angular movement as the joystick.

An electronic control has (from the electrical viewpoint) much in common with a servo except that it contains no electric motor. Pushing the joystick forward will increase r.p.m. proportionally to the movement (ahead, in this case). Move the joystick in the opposite direction and the same occurs, but then astern. With the joystick centred the motor is switched off.

Both servos and speed controls are fitted with plugs to connect them to the receiver, and are mounted in sturdy boxes.

6.31. This motor torpedo boat has a separate steerage motor coupled direct to the rudder shaft, i.e. without a steering arm (A. Bedet, NL).

Modern servos are about as large as a matchbox, speed controllers being a little larger at about 8.5 x 6 x 3.5 cm. Such dimensions mean that the rudder motor can be tucked away in a corner. They should, however, remain accessible to allow them to be transferred to another boat. It is, therefore, worthwhile making them removable, and thus transferable (assuming of course, that one uses the same type of control system). Usually 4-pin plugs are used to connect servo and controller to the receiver and these are usually polarised (i.e., can only be inserted one way round) to prevent mistakes. Similar plugs are used on the battery for the control system and the rudder servo.

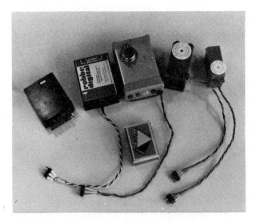

6.32. A 6-Channel receiver, speed control, a do-it-yourself speed control and two types of servo.

Such servos can not only steer the ship but also, by the addition of cams on either servo or steering rod, operate switches. As the joystick is moved a fraction the servo also turns. Hold the joystick stationary and the servo will stop, only to move again as the joystick is moved. There are actually two sorts of servo: one that describes an arc in moving backwards and forwards, and one that moves linearly (linear servo). A disc servo is an ideal control unit. If the cam on the servo disc is allowed to rotate past several switches, one servo can perform a number of functions (see Fig. 6.33). There are model builders who have equipped servos in their ship with 'programme discs' running up to no less than 14 functions (in fixed sequence). They switch lights on and off, operate search-lights and radar, set anchor winches, cranes and hoists working, or even cause smoke to emerge from the funnel. More of this in Chapter 9.

A number of manufacturers have introduced accessories that need only clipping onto the servo. Such consist of a small plate with a changeover switch on both sides. An eccentric servo disc that just fits between the switches operates them. One can use such a system to reverse the rotation of a motor and this is often done for the propulsion unit of small boats where there is no room to fit a speed control unit.

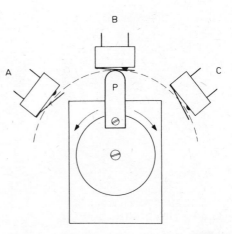

6.33. The cam mounted on the servo disc will operate the switches a, b, or c as it rotates.

A speed control unit can be used to operate multiple motors, provided that the total power capacity (shown on the control unit) is not exceeded. Otherwise there is a fair chance of the control burning out. Some speed control units have a built-in fuse, but even so it is well worth while fitting a fuse in the circuit in order to protect this expensive item. Double propellered ships can be fitted with two speed controls which allows one to steer with the propellers as well as with the rudder.

With all equipment, do stick to the manufacturer's instructions. Connect, too, in accordance with instructions in order to prevent damage to servos, speed control and battery. At this point one can reserve space in the hull for this equipment, it can then be fitted later without further ado. The hull must still be finished off and certainly while painting will be upside down so that any loose parts would fall out and be damaged. Only in the final stages of building should one fit the radio control system in its definite place. Following chapters will deal with connection of the varied equipment.

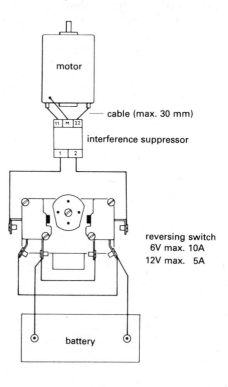

6.34   Reversing switch.

6.35. Two Monoperm Super motors with a 1:3 reduction and the proper screws combine to give this model a perfect scale speed (Wesselina, the author).

7 Energy sources and connections

By far the most scale models make use of electrical energy to drive the motors. This energy is supplied on board by dry cells, lead-acid batteries or nickel-cadmium cells. Other sorts, such as silver-zinc or silver-cadmium batteries can, of course, also be used. Here, apart from discussing the energy sources themselves, we will also consider their charging and means of connecting them and, further, the interference suppression of the propulsion motors. Two easy-to-read schematics for the propulsion motor will be found at the back of this book.

Dry cells

There are countless types of dry cell available and in nearly as many brands. They are a throw-away source of electrical energy for domestic equipment, portable radios, for example. Their great disadvantage is that they do not supply a constant voltage; during use the voltage falls off. The portable radio begins to sound hoarse and we know that it is time to fit new batteries. The old must be thrown away because they cannot be re-charged; one cannot reload them with energy.

If one uses such batteries as energy source for a model ship, it will sail fast enough to begin with but then the speed will drop sharply. The motor draws so much current that the pleasure of sailing is short and sweet. New batteries must be fitted which makes it a rather expensive hobby, certainly if one needs 6 or 8 of them.

As energy source for a reasonably sized model, dry cells do not therefore come into consideration. One could, perhaps, just use dry batteries in very small models during an F-6 or F-7 demonstration (see Chapter 12).

Dry batteries are just as ill-suited to the powering of the radio receiver. The receiver and certainly the servos will not operate effectively with a voltage below a certain value. With new batteries it is no problem, but they are quickly exhausted and one is left with an unsteerable ship.

For the transmitter, too, dry batteries are hardly used any more. The transmitter also requires a certain minimum voltage to function properly. In brief, the dry battery can be ignored as a source of power.

Lead-acid batteries

The best known form of rechargeable battery is the lead-acid battery. Large types are used in cars and motorcycles, where

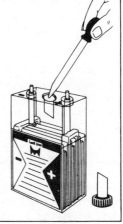

7.1. Well-known lead-acid batteries used to drive the motors in model ships.

7.2. Lead-acid batteries are filled with dilute sulphuric acid.

a dynamo charges them for further use. With models, they are charged with a battery charger.

Car batteries are obviously too large for use with models and certain manufacturers have, therefore, introduced model batteries that are suited to powering model ships. They are mostly rectangular glass or plastic boxes that are closed by a fixed lid. The lid is provided with holes for filling that are closed by ventilated plugs, either a push fit or screwed.

An accumulator is made up of specially prepared lead plates which are immersed in dilute sulphuric acid. (s.g. 1.24 – 1.28

127

or about 30%). When bought the accumulators are neither filled nor charged. Sulphuric acid can be acquired from a chemist and one can fill oneself using a funnel or laboratory pipette. The acid level should be just above the plates. Thereafter one can charge it in accordance with the maker's instructions (see further).

The dimensions of the battery differ depending on its voltage. Apart from the voltage the capacity is also stated. Capacity is expressed in ampere-hours, that is, the current in amperes x the duration in hours. With a battery of 4 ampere-hours (4 Ah) this means that the battery can (theoretically) deliver a current of 1 ampere for 4 hours. That means that if one's motor takes 1 ampere one can sail for 4 hours.

A battery must never be run completely down. This can cause the plates to deform and can even lead to an internal short-circuit, thus ruining the battery. The voltage per cell should never fall below 1.8 V (charged it is 2.5 V). Never exceed the current drain stated on the battery.

A 'normal' model battery, such as the Matshushita (6 V, 4 Ah) is about 90 x 40 x 60 mm (l x b x h). One can, of course, use more than one battery.

On the top of the battery are two terminals, a positive (+) and a negative (−) to which the electrical connections will be made, either by means of a screw in the threaded holes or, better still, by soldering. Always solder before the battery is filled. A little solder on the terminals will make it easier to make a connection later.

The voltage can be increased. By connecting the negative terminal of one battery to the positive terminal of another one can make a 12 V battery out of the two.

There are, of course, many types of battery. They differ in size, in capacity and in voltage. One can obtain 'wet' and 'dry' accumulators. Mostly sulphuric acid but there are also chloride and potassium that are wet and must be kept vertical, otherwise the aggressive electrolyte will escape.

Dry accumulators are also to be had under various brand names. They are all lead-acid batteries but in this case watertight, which makes them easy to install; they can also be mounted on their side (a survey of lead-acid batteries suitable for models will be found at the end of this book).

The acid level of wet accumulators needs to be checked from time to time. If the level falls below the top of the plates distilled water must be added.

Lead-acid batteries should be kept in a charged condition, even when not in use, once they are filled with acid. Unused batteries should, therefore, be charged once a month. If lead-acid batteries are left for any time uncharged and unused an insoluble layer forms on the plates which increases their internal resistance and renders them useless.

Lead-acid batteries are not used for transmitter and receiver. Apart from lead-acid batteries one can also obtain alkali batteries, the best known of which are the silver-zinc and the nickel-cadmium batteries. In place of acid they use an alkali as electrolyte. Their great advantage is that they need no maintenance such as charging when idle, and furthermore, they have a longer life than lead-acid batteries. They are light and can store more energy for a given weight than lead-acid batteries. There are also wet nickel-cadmium batteries which also have an alkaline electrolyte. Compared with the normal lead-acid batteries the alkaline types are pretty expensive, but are in the long term cheaper. The best known form is the dry nickel-cadmium type which is available for model use in the form of gas-tight cells.

Nickel-cadmium cells

Nickel-cadmium cells are commonly found in all sorts of portable equipment and are particularly suitable as power sources for model receivers and transmitters.

They can be had as button cells or as cylindrical cells. Both have a nominal voltage of 1.25 V. This means that several cells will be needed to power receivers and servos which mostly work on 4.8 V, four cells in series, therefore. For the transmitter even more will be needed because these work either on 9 V or 12 V. A survey of the various types is given at the end of this book.

The great advantages of these cells are: they are hermetically sealed, require no maintenance and have a life of about 1,000 charging cycles (say about 8 years). They have a low internal resistance which means that high currents can be delivered without damaging the cell. They are usable from − 30ºC to + 50ºC and have a flat voltage characteristic. What is meant by the last can be seen in the curves of Fig. 7.4. In these curves A is that of a normal dry cell and B the curve of a nickel-cadmium cell. The voltage of the nickel cell remains at a usable level for a long time whereas that of the dry cell drops off quite rapidly. In other words a battery of nickel-cadmium cells will maintain their voltage for a long period, which means that one can operate a model for long periods without loss of steerage. It depends, of course, on how fast the cells are discharged and that depends on the capacity.

7.3. Nickel-cadmium cells are often in the form of flat cylinders, commonly called button cells.

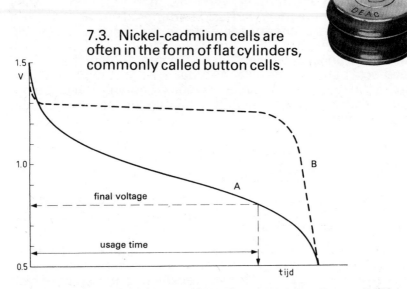

7.4. Voltage curve of a dry-cell (A) and a secondary cell (B). The charged voltage of the nickel-cadmium cell is about 1.25 V which remains more or less constant until the cell is almost fully discharged, when it falls off rapidly. By comparison the normal zinc-oxide cell has a higher initial voltage at 1.5 V but this falls rapidly until the end point of about 0.9 V is reached. The nickel-cadmium cell can, therefore, replace a dry-cell with advantage.

130

Capacity

With nickel-cadmium cells the capacity is expressed in milli-ampere-hours (mAh = 1/1 000 Ah, or, 1 Ah = 1,000 mAh). A nickel-cadmium cell with a capacity of 500 mAh can deliver 50 mA for 10 hours. The rate of discharge is expressed as the C-rate. The nominal capacity is valid for discharge in 5 hrs (C/5 in the curve of Fig. 7.6). Faster discharge reduces the capacity and slower discharge increases it.

Capacity is also temperature dependent, Fig. 7.7 shows that even at extreme temperatures a large part of the capacity is still available (nominal value is given at 20°C)

7.5. Another form of nickel-cadmium cell.

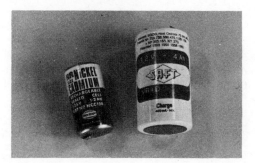

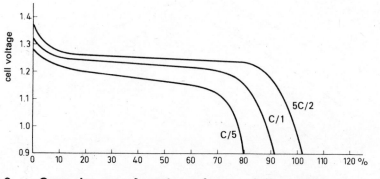

7.6.   Capacity as a function of rate of discharge.

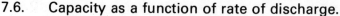

Sintered cells

For special applications one can use sintered nickel-cadmium cells (both button and cylindrical) that can deliver a very high current for short periods without incurring damage, and without noticeable loss of voltage. This type of cell is often used for racing. For some minutes a very high current is drawn from the cells to supply a current-devouring motor that is running virtually red-hot at an extremely high r.p.m.

Each brand codes sintered cells in their own way, for example, DEAC identify sintered cells as DKZ, SAFT as RS and VR.

Using Nickel-Cadmium cells as batteries

An important property of nickel-cadmium cells is their low internal resistance. Some examples are given below of the common batteries used in model sailing from the firms Varta (DEAC) and CGE (SAFT):

DEAC DK 450, capacity 450 mAh: r_i = 0.25 Ohms appr.
DEAC DKZ 500, capacity 500 mAh: r_i = 0.08 Ohms appr.
SAFT VB 50, capacity 550 mAh: r_i = 0.05 Ohms appr.

For the receiver we will, therefore, choose a DKZ 500 or a VB 50. For a model with several servos and associate functions a normal battery would be too quickly exhausted. One would then choose a higher capacity battery (up to 1,200 mAh) from the ranges of SAFT, Berec or General Electric.

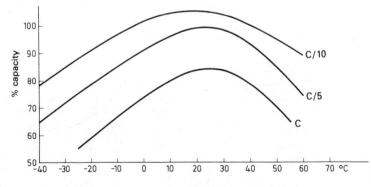

7.7.   Capacity as a function of temperature.

Most manufacturers of radio control equipment include a 500 mAh battery (weight about 116 g), but if one needs to be careful about weight (which doesn't often happen with boats) one can manage with a 225 mAh battery (about 50 g) provided one only uses one or two servos.

If one wants to sail for a long period then one can better use a battery of 1,000 mAh (about 235 g). In the transmitter a type DK battery is suitable (slightly higher internal resistance) because no load peaks occur. Sintered cells are, by the way, a little dearer than the DK batteries.

Nickel-cadmium cells require no maintenance; you can forget them for months at a time and just charge them up before use. The batteries do self-discharge during storage, say 25% in the

7.8. The tugboat Aegir (Dutch Champion in the F2A class in 1976) uses 7 Ah nickel-cadmium batteries as power source. (H.K.J. v.d. Bussche, NL).

first month and 10 – 15% per month thereafter. One should, therefore, recharge before using after they have been stored for three weeks or more.

If a nickel-cadmium battery is not fully charged (particularly that of the receiver) the radio control starts acting up. Servos start operating when not commanded to, and the speed control switches the motor from ahead to astern.

Certainly 30% of radio control troubles can be laid at the door of incorrectly (and insufficiently) charged batteries; there is either a dud cell (change it) or the battery is charged up the wrong way (in which case recharge it the right way).

133

Charging batteries

To charge batteries one needs a battery charger; one can't just connect them to the mains. The mains voltage must be transformed to a lower voltage and must be converted from alternating current to direct current. The charger should supply a somewhat higher voltage than the nominal voltage of the battery it must charge.

A number of battery chargers are available that are specially designed for model batteries. One can buy them in the model shop. Although these chargers are suitable for charging lead-acid batteries it is worthwhile getting a car battery charger. These have charging currents from about 500 mA to 5 or

7.9.   A multi-charger.

10 A, which is useful when one considers that some lead-acid batteries must be charged at 1 A or more. Small lead-acid batteries or 'dry' batteries can be charged with the normal model charger.

Nickel-cadmium batteries should be always charged up on the (multi) charger. Such a charger has various current ranges and several batteries can be charged simultaneously, apart from the fact that nickel-cadmium cells should be charged at a constant current, that current should be 10% of the capacity of the battery. With this type of battery charger the charging current is either adjustable or one can choose from various values. Small batteries can be charged at voltages from 2 to 12 V.

Examples of the various charging currents that are available on such a charger are: 1 x 10 mA/1 x 22 mA (sometimes 1 x 25 mA)/ 2 x 50 mA/1 x 100 mA (sometimes 1 x 50 mA and 2 x 100 mA, it depends on the make) and 1 x 500 mA. When the highest value is used the others may not be used simultaneously. When one of the current ranges is in use a lamp lights. With complete sets of nickel-cadmium batteries special charging cables are supplied. The one wire is red the other black, at one end they have a plug that fits in the socket on the battery and on the other two banana plugs that fit the

7.10.　A multi-meter.

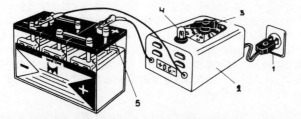

7.11.　A battery must be charged in the right way:
　　　　1 mains connection, 2 battery charger, 3 control knob,
　　　　4 warning lamp, 5 crocodile clips.

135

7.12. Charging cable
as used for the
receiver battery.

7.13. Servo extension cable.

sockets on the charger. The sockets on the charger are marked with their polarity; never interchange positive and negative – it will cost you batteries. There are usually three connections to the battery: a red, a blue (or black) and a white (or
yellow), the last of which is a centre tap, required for servos
and receivers.

Charging the batteries is child's play. One removes the filler
plugs and connects the battery to the charger via about 30 or
40 cm of wire ($2\frac{1}{2}$ mm²), (the one red, the other black or blue),
on the one end crocodile clips and the other a banana plug.
One can read on the battery just what the charging current
should be and for how long.

Charging times

A good voltmeter is an advantage but, as you have seen in
Chapter 6, it is also advantageous to be able to measure
currents, so a multi-meter is much better. If one connects the
meter to a battery on charge (don't forget the polarity) you
will see that it indicates 6 V or more. Lead-acid batteries
(including the dry variety) should be charged to $1\frac{1}{4}$ x the
nominal voltage – a 6 V battery should, therefore, be charged
to $1\frac{1}{4}$ x 6 V = 7.5 V. At this point the battery is fully charged,
something one can hear from the bubbling of the electrolyte.
Don't let it bubble too long as it is not good for the battery and
the gases released are explosive. Replace the filler plugs and
the battery is ready for use.

When purchased, nickel-cadmium batteries always need
charging. With DEAC batteries this is 14 hours at the stated
current. It differs from make to make, but one should always
stick to the instructions that come with the battery. The

multi-meter can be used (just as with a lead-acid battery) to measure the voltage. Because the batteries are usually not completely flat after use, 14 hours is unnecessarily long for recharging, but just in what state of discharge they are is difficult to tell. A good rule of thumb is to give them one hour's charge for every 15 minutes discharge they have had. Thus if one has operated the ship for one hour, you should charge the batteries for four hours. When you are not certain, charge the batteries to 1 1/5 x their nominal voltage; for a 4.8 V battery to 1 1/5 x 4.8 = 5.75 V. One must never exceed 1.45 V per cell.

Provided one doesn't exceed the stated charging current a certain amount of overcharging isn't a disaster (apart from DEAC button cells which are damaged by overcharging), but don't make a habit of it because it isn't good for the life of the batteries. Nickel-cadmium cells are flat when the voltage has dropped to 1.1 V per cell; for a four cell battery, therefore, to 4.4 V. A lower charging current may always be used provided that the charging time is proportionately extended.

Wiring and connections.

To get the electrical energy from the source to the users one requires electrical conductors – one really does have to pull a few wires. At the radio dealer or the surplus stores (where you can at the same time look round for switches and suchlike that will be useful for model building) one can buy wire in all diameters and colours. It is best to buy a couple of colours in each size, particularly in red, orange, black and blue, with perhaps yellow and green. Red is always the positive with black or blue as negative. The other colours are suitable for secondary connections. Buy flexible stranded wire, not the sort with a single solid conductor – one nick when stripping and the wire will soon break from the vibration of the ship. For the heavier loads use wire with a cross-sectional area of $2\frac{1}{2}$ mm², such as is used in cars. Thinner wire with a c.s.a. of $\frac{1}{2}$ mm² can be used for extending servo connections, but stick to the colour already used to prevent mistakes.

Where possible solder the wires to the terminals using resin-cored solder. One can solder in the following way. Bare the end of the wire and twist the strands together. Switch on the soldering iron and wait until it is at the right temperature.

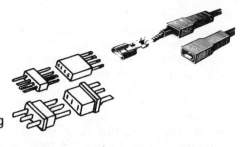

7.14. Various connecting plugs and sockets.

Touch the end of the solder against the wire and bring both into contact with the tip of the soldering iron. The solder will melt and run over the wire. Remove from the soldering iron and the solder will harden in several seconds. Do the same with the terminal to which the wire is to be soldered. Both are now tinned. Should the terminal be oxidised, use a little sand-paper to remove the oxide.

Never use one of the active fluxes as they attack copper in time, especially not with printed wiring boards (to which components are mounted). Finally, bring the wire in contact with the terminal and touch the soldering iron against both. The solder will flow together and give you an excellent contact. Don't move the wire until the solder has hardened. Once hard the solder should have a shiny surface; if it is dull and crumbly it shows that the connection will break off in use.

With some plugs the two terminals are so close together that they can easily touch and, furthermore, the casing is of plastic that melts if it gets too hot. The best thing is to hold the body in a vice (which frees both your hands as well). Having soldered the wires and checked that there is no contact, slip a little insulating sleeving over the joints. Use solder always sparingly, avoiding blobs. The tip of the iron should be tapered for fine work. An iron of 25 or 40 watts is big enough for most of the work encountered. One can also make the connections using banana plugs and sockets which can be had from the model shop in a variety of colours. Even simpler are the clip-on contacts used in cars, which one can obtain from an accessory shop. At radio dealers one can also buy special plugs and sockets but they are more expensive.

In the boat the various wires are bundled neatly together; it not only makes everything easier to find, it also prevents faults, and a lot of hunting when one does have a fault. The

138

components, themselves, are virtually 100% sound. It is the 'mechanic' who often makes a mess of things.

Tidy wiring

Apart from making the wiring tidy one should also keep it as short as possible. A short direct connection between battery, reversing switch, speed control and motor is better than a roundabout route between source and load. Because the current doesn't have to travel so far the losses are less and there is less chance of electrical interference from the motor wiring. Interference can be so bad that it affects the control of the boat. Where possible one should keep the wiring of the motor separate from that of the servos and receiver. The one on the port side and the other on the starboard, for example, Fig. 7.15 gives an impression of a built-in set. DIN plugs and sockets are used here and the wiring is carried through the superstructure (here removed) to the main switch for motor and radio control.

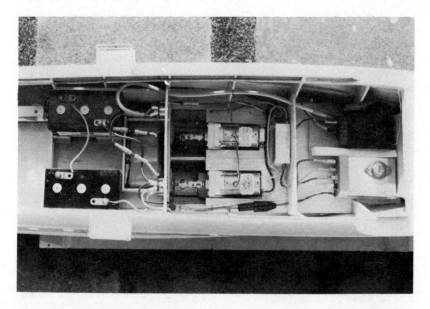

7.15.   Installation and wiring of motors, receiver, batteries and speed control. The wiring systems are kept apart. (M.S. Wesselina).

It is often worth while having a single main switch. Everything is either on or off and there is no chance of forgetting to switch off one or other part with the consequent battery drain. Many radio installations have a built-in slide switch and if one doesn't want (or dare) to fit another, one should at least switch both the positive and negative supply lines. One can fit the switches below decks but then one has to remove the superstructure to get at them. One can always hide them above decks, under a hatch or a chest or even under a coil of rope. There are plenty of suitable small switches about and with a bit of trouble and handiness one can usually find a solution.

Antenna wire should not be laid anyhow over supply wires and apparatus. Make an antenna of thin steel wire or copper rod and connect it with as short a wire as possible, using a special antenna plug and socket. And make the antenna the same length as advised by the manufacturer of the radio control.

One can hide an antenna of copper wire (from an old coil or transformer) among the rigging. Don't try to use the railing because an antenna needs to be more or less vertical. The length of an antenna varies between about 60 and 80 cm. Ships with a 'high' hull and superstructure enable one to lose some of the antenna within the hull, if it is wood or plastic. With warships it is fairly easy and, in any case, the antenna that does protrude is barely noticeable among all the antennae and rigging that they must have.

Small electrically driven functions can be operated by a small tumbler switch instead of by a servo. These switches are often found on servos as reversing switches and are often used in the motor circuit.

Fig. 7.18 shows how a secondary switch can be placed unobtrusively on deck. Use is made here of bronze rod and tube,

7.16. Types of banana plug and switches.

very versatile components in model building and the model shop has choice enough.

Fusing

Certainly the motor, but if possible all other current-using parts should be fused. Keep the fuse value to the lowest possible. For example, if the motor draws 3.1 A, then fit a fuse of 3.5 A (3,500 mA) and not 6 A. If your propeller ever gets

7.17. The receiving antenna is concealed in the superstructure. (A64, Ruhr, G.Rudolph, BRD).

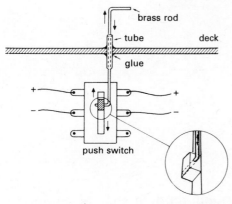

7.18.   A concealed switch.

7.19. The capacitance of the capacitors used depends on the type of motor.

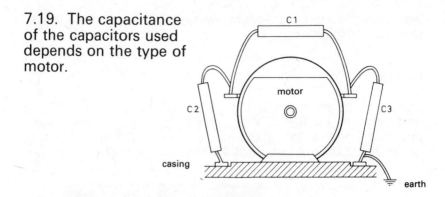

entangled in water plants it is better that the motor stops than that it burns out!

Interference suppression of electric motors

One of the greatest problems in using electric motors is getting rid of the electrical interference they cause. With Marx motors it is often sufficient to solder interference suppression capacitors across the motor terminals. In radio component shops one can buy capacitors and ferrite beads for interference suppression. They cost little and it is worth buying more than you need; there will always be other motors that need to be suppressed. One needs capacitors of 47,000 pF (pico-Farad) and 0.1μF (micro-Farad). You can see in Fig. 7.19 how

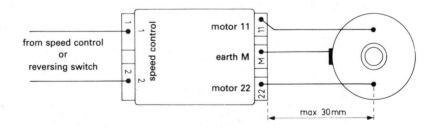

7.20. Complete suppression module that is connected direct to the motor.

142

they should be connected; always keep the capacitor leads as short as possible.

If the terminals of the motor are too small then one can always use the metal parts out of connector blocks (chocolate blocks). After fitting the capacitors and the beads one pushes one end of the terminal (from the connector block) over the motor terminal and screws it fast. If necessary one can solder it as well. The supply leads can then be pushed in the other end of the terminal and screwed tight. In Fig. 7.20 you will see that the motor housing is earthed. This is something one should always do because a lot of interference problems can be prevented by good earthing.

One must add that proper interference suppression is often a matter of trial and error. One motor is, in this respect, easier than another.

8 Finishing off the scale model

One can with confidence say that there is no part of model building which gives more rein to creativity than the super-structure. Apart from the moving parts the numberless variations in hoists, winches, cranes, cutters, radar and antenna, masts, rigging, guns and fire hydrants offer sufficient opportunity for invention. Detail and finish determine the appearance of the model and one cannot be too detailed. One can even build a prototype down to the last rivet.

In order to give food for thought, and because it is difficult to describe each and every part of the superstructure, this chapter contains more illustrations than text. When building a

8.1. Upper deck of the tugboat Sun (K.A. Gramende NL).

8.2 Fender on the Moorcock.

scale model it is advisable to get hold of as much literature and original drawings as one can. It is also worth while visiting maritime museums both at home and abroad. Borrow books if possible from public libraries or museums, and it goes without saying that you will make use of your camera in ports and harbours. Before we discuss the details of the superstructure there is one technique that is virtually indispensable.

Silver-soldering

We have spoken of soldering in the previous chapter and here we made use of a soft solder with a low melting point (between 200 and 400°C). Apart from electrical connections one can also use it for other joints but it is not particularly strong, especially where the areas to be joined are small. The use of a silver-solder gives a much stronger connection than with soft solder. It is a very different alloy.

Use is made of silver-solder when making propeller or supports for (internal combustion) engines where the strength requirements are high.

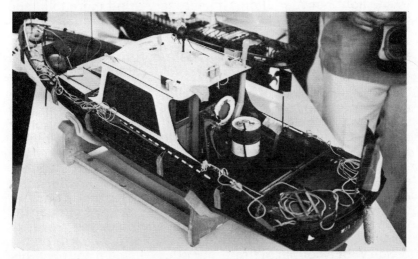

8.3. One can never have too much detail (M. Pfannenstein, BRD).

Silver-solder is an alloy of silver, copper, zinc and cadmium, of which the melting point lies between 600 and 900°C. This temperature is, of course, above that of a soldering iron. With silver-soldering, in any case, one needs to heat a much greater area of the surfaces to be joined, which is beyond the capabilities of an iron. For silver-soldering use is made of a burner. There are plenty to choose from in the shops, but make sure that you don't choose one too small. There is

145

nothing more disheartening than discovering that you can't get the job hot enough.

For silver-soldering one uses a form of flux which when heated becomes treacly and prevents the formation of oxides on the joint that would otherwise interfere with the solder uniting with the metals to be joined.

The method

Ensure that the surfaces to be joined are free from oxides, dirt and grease and mate nicely together. One should not be able to see light between them; if necessary grind them to shape by rubbing the two parts together with a little grinding paste in between.

Having removed the grinding paste and having degreased the surfaces one is ready to hard solder them.

One takes two pieces of iron wire (fine) about half a metre long and twists them together, with the help of a hand drill, if necessary. This wire is used to bind the two parts together without letting the iron wire contact the surfaces to be joined. Particularly with small work-pieces the iron wire prevents the flame blowing them away. With everything in place we take some flux. This has probably been bought in powder form and needs making up with a little water. At the same time we cut pieces of hard solder a few millimetres long. Smear the joint abundantly with the flux paste and place the pieces of solder as close as you can to the joint. Form a hearth on the bench with a couple of fire-proof bricks, using a couple more to make a back wall and a side wall. The work piece is then placed about 5 cm from the corner that is so formed. The burner is then lighted and adjusted so that a clear blue-violet cone can be seen (it is an advantage if the ambient light isn't too strong). The work-piece is now brought to temperature. Once the whole is red-hot one brings the blue-violet cone (the hottest part of the flame) to bear on the joint. The bits of solder will suddenly melt and run through the joint like mercury. If it doesn't entirely fill the joint then apply more heat to the area where you want the solder to go. This sort of solder has the tendency to run where it is hottest. Once the entire joint is filled you are finished: if not, you have either used too little solder or the joint wasn't properly clean.

146

In the first case one can use tweezers or suchlike to add solder and then to reheat. In the second case the only thing to do is part the pieces (hot) and begin again, which means removing all the solder. Once one has got the hang of it it is not too difficult and you will be able to judge just how much solder you need for a given joint.

One must bear a couple of things in mind: that all metal becomes soft with heat, so don't use good tools in the flame; to add extra solder stick to one pair of tweezers, otherwise they'll all be as soft as putty. When warming up the work-piece try to do it evenly because it will then cool off evenly. If it doesn't, uneven contraction may cause the joint to break. If you find it later necessary to solder something to a part where you have already made a joint you can either use one of the thermally insulating pastes that can be obtained or you can stick the part to be cool in a piece of potato.

To prevent oxidisation forming on parts of the workpiece other than where one is soldering, cover it with flux. The work-piece can be allowed to cool off or one can quench in cold water. This last makes copper alloys softer, but steel is made harder and can become too brittle for further work. In this case heat the piece again until the *oxide layer* (not the steel itself) is blue to red (depending on the steel). This is known as softening or de-tempering. Quenching has the advantage that the glass-hard layer of flux breaks off due to the sudden contraction. It you let the work-piece cool off slowly you will have to remove this layer with a steel brush or glass-paper (not with a file – the layer is too hard).

Hard-soldering aluminium

Until recently hard-soldering aluminium was considered to be virtually impossible (at least for the amateur). Now there are systems using a special flux that enable excellent results to be obtained.

One must certainly watch which sort of aluminium one uses because some of them contain so much magnesium that they burn like a torch. This sort is often used by printers so watch out for scraps of unknown origin. First heat up a piece as big as a matchstick to see if it is all right.

Hard-soldering with aluminium doesn't differ much from other hard-soldering except that the oxide layer forms very rapidly. This layer prevents the solder uniting with the surface unless special measures are taken.

There are several ways of preventing an oxide layer forming and your supplier will be able to advise you which to use and how to use it, and once you've mastered silver-soldering with other metals there is no reason why you should not also master aluminium. One thing is, however, a nuisance and that is that the melting point of aluminium differs very little from that of the solder. Unless one is very careful in applying the heat one is likely to be left with an ugly blob instead of a beautiful piece of work.

8.4. The Admiral Scheer has a 'planked' deck (H.Muster, BRD).

The deck

At the end of Chapter 5 we had reached a point with the hull when we could start thinking about the superstructure. First the deck must be fitted (in accordance with the drawing), but before doing this make sure that there are no spaces beneath decks in which switches or other equipment must be fitted and which you are now going to close off. By fitting hatches we make these places accessible; one place that must be kept free in this way is the deck above the rudder.

Decks can be kept smooth in imitation of a steel deck or can be planked. In model shops one can buy wood panels in which grooves have been milled. These are obtainable with various widths of plank. If you want to do it completely yourself you will have to buy veneer from which planks are cut and which are cemented one by one to the deck. Some model builders have done this with up to 3,000 (!) planks of $50 \times 4 \times 0.5$ mm. One can, of course, just draw the planks on the deck, first in pencil and then in indian ink. Such a deck can be seen in Fig. 8.4.

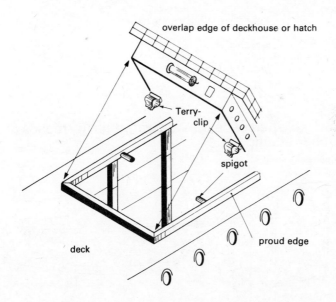

overlap edge of deckhouse or hatch

Terry-clip

spigot

deck

proud edge

8.5.   The deckhouse fits over a protruding edge.

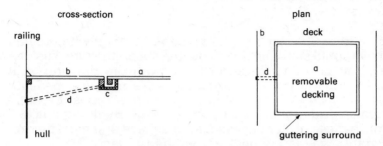

8.6. Separate section of deck (a) rests in a gutter (c); (b) is part of the fixed deck. One can provide (c) with a drain pipe (d) provided everything is enclosed.

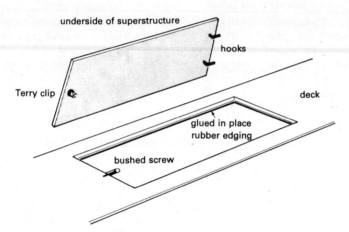

8.7. Removable part of deck made watertight by means of a rubber edging.

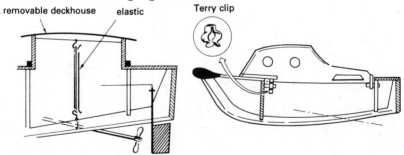

8.8. Some suggestions for fixing a deckhouse.

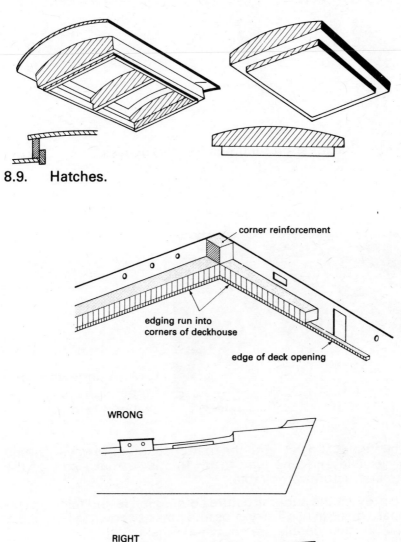

8.9. Hatches.

corner reinforcement

edging run into
corners of deckhouse

edge of deck opening

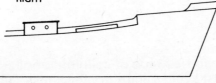

WRONG

RIGHT

8.10. Strengthening the corners and positioning of a deckhouse.

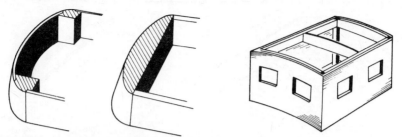

8.11. Construction methods for deckhouses.

8.12. Windows in a frame of brass section (Jason).

The radio control and the batteries must always remain accessible and one way to do this is to make part of the superstructure removable.

To prevent the superstructure coming loose and falling over-board one can use Terry clips and pins as shown in Figs. 8.5, 6 & 7. Further details are shown in Figs. 8.8. to 8.11.

Windows

The windows can be made of celluloid or of stiff transparent plastic of at least a half millimetre thickness. One cements the window to the inside of the deckhouse and makes it fast by means of a frame, also on the inside. One can also make a

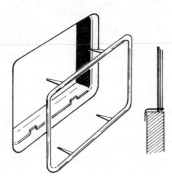

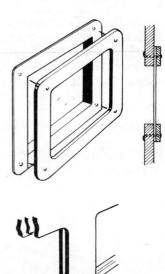

8.13.   Ways to mount windows.

double wall and slip the window between the walls, making the glass fast with metal or wood strips which can be screwed or nailed in place. One must ensure that no cement is forced out of the joint between window and frame. The windows must remain free of cement, scratches or other disfigurements (see Fig. 8.13). Sometimes complete windows are supplied with the kit.

Lighting

In fitting lighting in the deck-houses one can make use of bicycle lamp bulbs with their fittings (6 V, 0.05 A), fixed at various places in the hull. These give enough light to shine through the windows but one must leave the deck open within the deck-houses. See Fig. 8.14. One also gets light below decks and if a further upper deck is to be fitted one can make the floor of that open so that the light shines through to above. In this way a couple of lamps are enough to light the whole ship. If the scale is large and the windows and portholes consequently large one must ensure that the lamps cannot be seen from outside.

Navigation and deck lights

Real looking navigation and deck lights can be made using 3 V miniature lamps that are obtainable from the model shop.

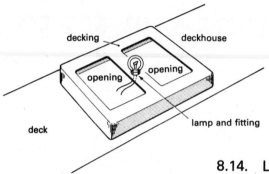

8.14. Lighting deckhouses.

One can see from the working drawing where the lights should be fitted and if no suitable holders are supplied with the kit then one can either buy them separately or make them oneself, from bronze tube, for example. If the masts are also made of bronze tube the lamp holders can be soldered to the mast together with the negative supply wire, the positive then being brought down inside the mast. This way one gets fewer (ugly) supply lines running over the ship. Navigation lights can be fitted in the same way (see Fig. 8.15).

The lower end of the mast fits in the superstructure somewhere and at this point one can connect it to the negative supply. Several lamps may be fitted to the mast and can either have one common positive supply line, in which case they are connected in parallel and are all on at the same time. Alternatively they can have separate supply lines (if there is room for them in the mast). With very small scales (1:125 or 1:150) the lamps will be too large and one will have to build them in partially. Another way is to use model railway lamps, but the light level is, of course, lower.

In principle navigation lights are green for starboard, red for port, with one or two white lights at the top of the mast; a white light also shows astern and then there are the anchor light and the bow light. Depending on type and function ships may carry a fair number of lights, but in most cases they will be shown in the drawings.

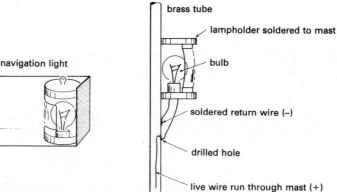

navigation light

brass tube

lampholder soldered to mast

bulb

soldered return wire (−)

drilled hole

live wire run through mast (+)

8.15.   Navigation lights.

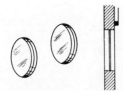

8.16.   Portholes.

Port-holes and doors

Sometimes the kit will include complete portholes, including 'glass'. They can also be made from hollow rivets or by the more labour-intensive method shown here (Fig. 8.17). Many ships have a sort of 'eyebrow' above the porthole which can be made of iron or copper wire. The window itself can be of cement or, with larger diameters, of circles of celluloid cut out of sheet with a piece of hollow tube (Figs. 8.17 to 8.19).

155

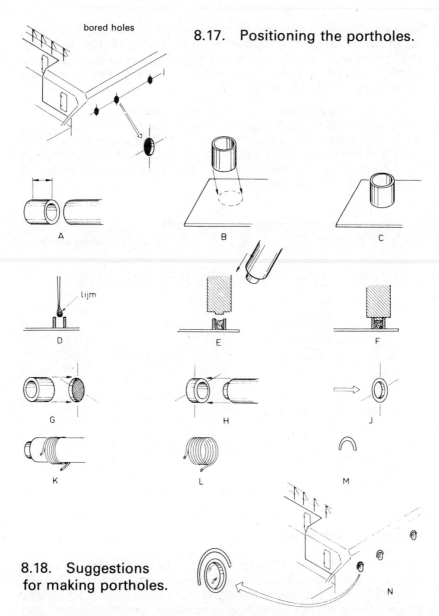

bored holes

8.17.   Positioning the portholes.

A

B

C

lijm

D

E

F

G

H

J

K

L

M

8.18.   Suggestions for making portholes.

N

With some scales a contour is sufficient and these are cut out of sheet as above and are cemented in place. This is less laborious than the glass and tube method.

156

8.19. Punching 'glass' for the portholes.

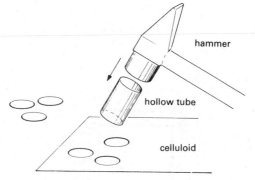

hammer

hollow tube

celluloid

8.20. Portholes and deck doors on the tugboat Aegir.

Doors (incl. water-tight doors)

Apart from ordinary doors of metal or wood, with or without porthole, warships have water-tight doors of the type shown Fig. 8.21 A and B. Hinges and closing clamps are usually in a separate flange round the door. In warships, doors of type A are held water-tight (and sometimes gas-tight) by means of clamps. Hinges can be either internal or external.

157

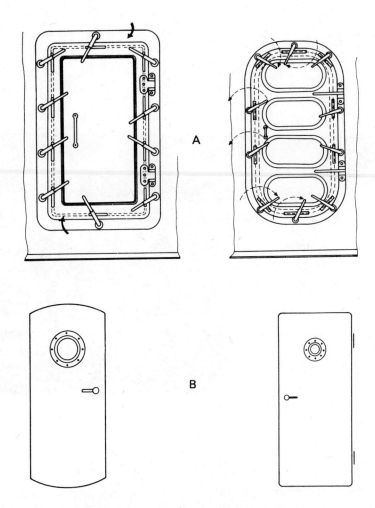

8.21. Watertight and ordinary doors.

8.22.   Details of the Swedish ship Gina (Billing Boats).

Railings

Railings and suchlike can be bought ready to use, but if one decides to do it oneself then many ready-made parts can be bought. Brass stanchions have holes at regular intervals so that fine brass or copper wire can be threaded through. At intervals the wire and the stanchions are soldered together to create a sturdy railing. In place of wire one can also use fine chain (Fig. 8.23).

If one is going to make everything oneself then the stanchions should be made from brass tubing (1½ to 2 mm dia. for scale 1:25 and larger), holes being bored through the tubing so that the wire or chain can be threaded through.

For this one can make a jig of the same length as the stanchions and with pre-bored holes. One should bear in mind that part of the stanchions is hidden in the deck. The stanchions should be an exact fit in the jig. By drilling the holes in the stanchions through the jig one ensures that they are equidis-

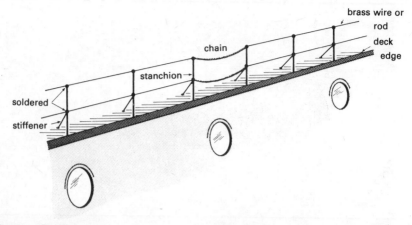

8.23. Railings.

tant in all stanchions. If the jig is properly clamped under a drill holder the holes will be perpendicular. (See Fig. 8.24).

8.24. Drilling stanchions.

Gangways and ladders

Gangways and ladders are either supplied with the kit or they can be bought separately. They are either of brass or plastic. Should one wish to make them oneself then one should use the method described here; it is commonly used and is shown in Fig. 8.25.

One makes a jig of hardwood not quite so broad as the treads. At the correct angle (50 to 55°) one makes sawcuts at the same intervals as the treads which are deep enough for a half of the

160

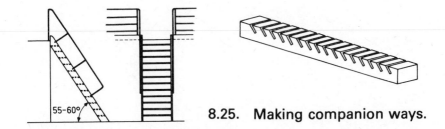

8.25. Making companion ways.

tread. One slips treads (of plastic, for example) in the jig and cements the side-pieces in place. It is best to make them in situ, thus ensuring that they fit perfectly. Plastic gangways are the easiest; they are easily cemented and can be easily cut to size. Metal gangways can be soldered.

Ladders

The best way to make ladders is to use thin soft copper or brass wire. The longitudinal members are made fast to a piece of wood at a distance from each other as required by the scale. At right angles to these one lays copper wire so as to

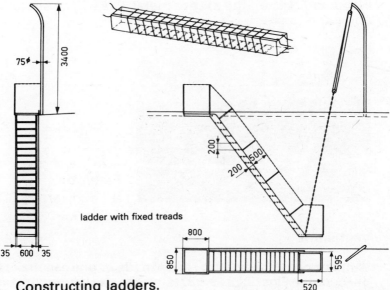

ladder with fixed treads

8.26. Constructing ladders.

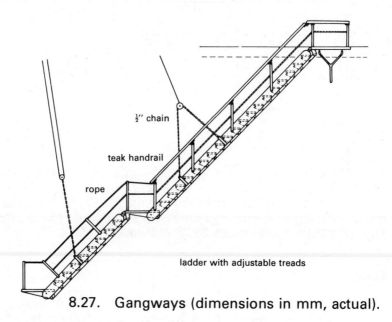

teak handrail

½" chain

rope

ladder with adjustable treads

8.27. Gangways (dimensions in mm, actual).

create rungs which can be soldered to the longitudinal members. One carefully removes the ladder from the block of wood and cuts off the excess metal. File off the sharp edges and cut it to size.

8.28. Gangway of the Potemkin (H. Schwarzer, DDR).

Ventilators

Ventilators can be bought ready-made or one can make them oneself, see Figs. 8.29 to 8.32. One can use cardboard, copper or tin. When using cardboard one should finish the part with lacquer or cement to prevent if fluffing.

Funnels

The shape and position of the funnel, or funnels, depending on the type of ship, is fixed by the working drawing. Some funnels are part of other superstructure, others not. In warships they are either part of the superstructure or they are

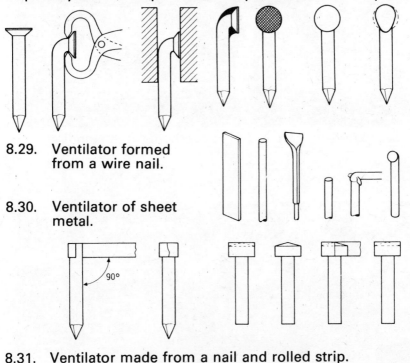

8.29. Ventilator formed from a wire nail.

8.30. Ventilator of sheet metal.

8.31. Ventilator made from a nail and rolled strip.

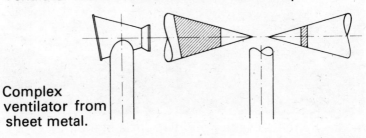

8.32. Complex ventilator from sheet metal.

8.33. Funnels, here of the F51 Ashanti (free-standing).

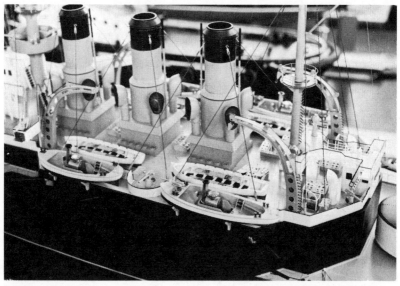

8.34. Funnels of the Potemkin (free-standing).

164

8.35. Admiral Scheer: funnels as part of the superstructure.

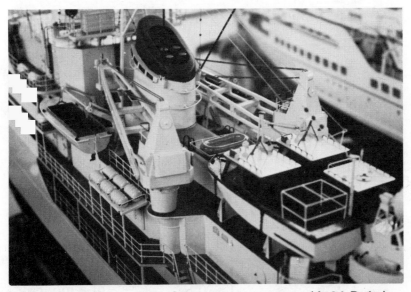

8.36. Funnels as part of the superstructure (A 64 Ruhr).

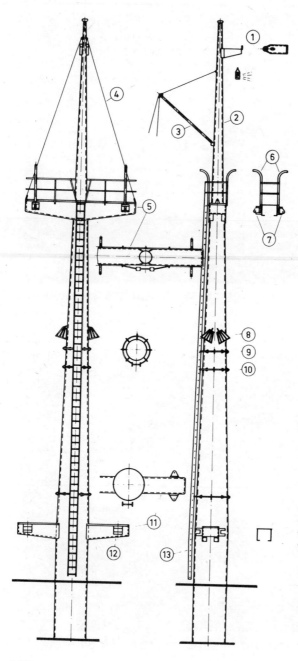

1. lamp bracket
2. topmast
3. gaff
4. shrouds
5. cross-trees
6. davit
7. topping-lift pad
8. lamp cage
9. handrail
10. footrail
11. mast-table
12. gooseneck bearing
13. ladder

8.37. Example of the mast of a modern ship.

166

surrounded by searchlights or defensive weapons. Steam pipes are sometimes found in older ships, but with modern ships these are hidden within the funnel and one can only see their ends. The smoke, gas and ventilation channels of auxiliary motors, tanks and bunkers may be also so hidden.

If the funnel is hollow one can fit a smoke generator (see Chapter 9). In some cases one will find a pre-prepared or ready-to-use funnel in the kit. Various photographs in this book contain examples of different forms of funnel.

Masts, antennae and rigging

The requisite material for the masts is usually to be found in the kit – usually a set of wooden sticks. You can certainly build a mast with it but very little more. In any case the wood usually warps! It is better to make a mast oneself from brass

8.38. Masts and rigging amidships on the French warship Richelieu (W. Stresse, BRD, 1975 Champion in Class FZC).

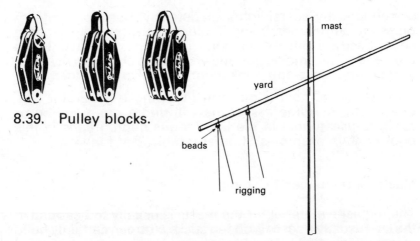

8.39. Pulley blocks.

8.40. Beads used for tackle from a yard.

tube and rod. It is easy to solder which means that one can fix anenometers, lights, antennae and radar. One can, of course, also use epoxy cement and for very small parts cyano-acrylate cement.

One can best make antennae from brass rod or, with wire antennae, from fine copper wire. If you use enamelled wire

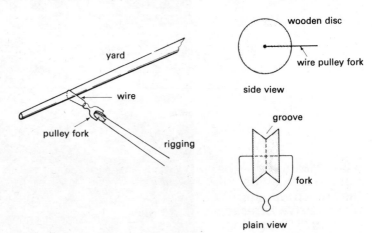

8.41. Making and fixing pulley blocks.

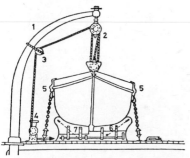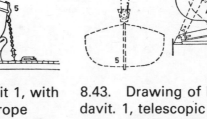

8.42. Arm of davit 1, with block 2, pulley 3, rope brake 4, clamps 5, and keel clamps 6,7.

8.43. Drawing of hinged davit. 1, telescopic arm, 2, davit arm, 3, rest position, 4, lowering position, 5, boat lowering by rope through tackle, 6.

8.44. Completely rigged freighter Badenstein (W. Lehmann, BRD).

8.45.   Launch and jolly boat in the davits.

you must remember to scrape away the enamel where you need to solder. When copper wire is used it is easy to disguise the antenna of the radio control receiver.

Antennae and rigging can also be made of white or black iron wire and nylon fishing line (very difficult to knot). With larger models use is also made of black elastic (obtainable from the haberdasher's).

One can bind rigging and antennae to the mast or, what looks better, make use of a real block and tackle (Fig. 8.39). They can be bought in various types and sizes, but only in certain scales, for example 1:200; even these are too large. One can also fit beads to the yards and masts. A little cement is enough to keep them in place and one can thread the rigging or antenna through the holes (Fig. 8.40).

If the scale permits, it is, of course, always better to use genuine blocks. If they are large enough you can make them yourself and, as can be seen from Fig. 8.41, a lot can be done with a little wire and wooden rod.

8.46. Lifeboats, davits and cranes on the freighter Badenstein.

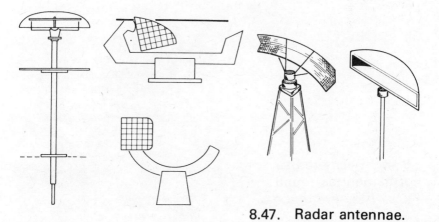

8.47. Radar antennae.

171

Cranes, hoists and davits

One can fit stationary cranes and hoists or, where the scale permits, one can fit ones that actually work. Bearings can be made from brass tubes fitting one within the other, and hinges can be made from ordinary hooks and eyes. Any ropes used must actually run through the pulley blocks and can be wound up on a winch. The method used we leave to the reader because it is something to which everyone will prefer to find his own solution.

Davits are mostly used to support lifeboats and should be so made that they can be turned outboard and extended ready for lowering. Figs. 8.42 and 8.43 show some types of davit. They can be made of brass and/or wood but are often found ready made in the kit.

Radar

Radar antennae can be made of metal gauze with a piece of bronze wire soldered round the circumference. This makes them look better and prevents the edges from becoming untidy. Harbour or navigation radar antennae can be made from some sorts of razor blade holder; if a hole is drilled one can cement in a shaft to make it rotatable. Simple radar antennae can be seen in Fig. 8.47. They can be mounted on a platform or on a tripod.

8.48. Ready-to-use armament as found in kits. They are made of wood and plastic.

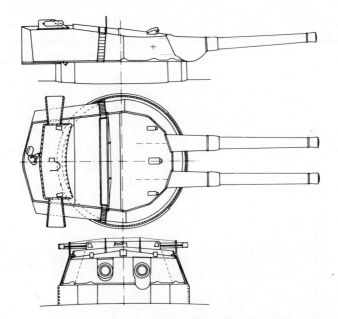

8.49.   English gun turret.

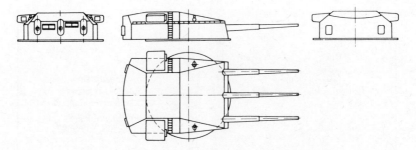

8.50.   German gun turret.

Warship armament

While on the subject of warships it is worth saying something about their armament, to which one could actually devote an entire book. A great body of literature exists, not so much

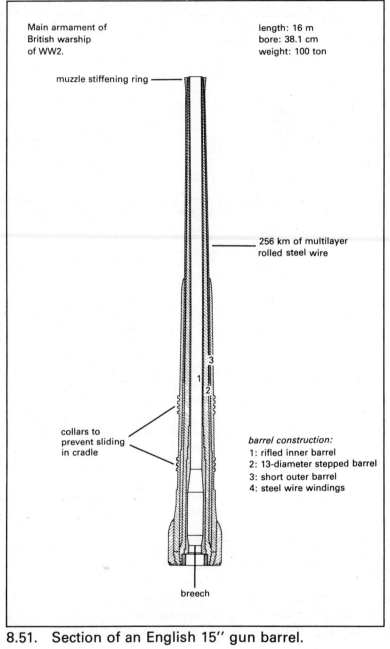

Main armament of
British warship
of WW2.

length: 16 m
bore: 38.1 cm
weight: 100 ton

muzzle stiffening ring ——

256 km of multilayer
rolled steel wire

3
1
2

collars to
prevent sliding
in cradle

barrel construction:
1: rifled inner barrel
2: 13-diameter stepped barrel
3: short outer barrel
4: steel wire windings

breech

8.51.   Section of an English 15'' gun barrel.

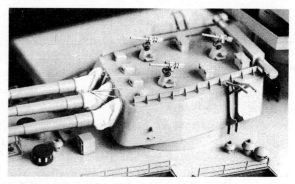

8.52. The 15″ gun barrels in the courtyard of the Imperial War Museum in London come from the old British warships Ramillies and Resolution. (Photo. I.W.M., London).

8.53. Rear turret of the Russian warship Oktyabrskaya Revolutsia (see also Fig. 3.18.).

over models as over the original ships. But even these offer considerable help to the model builder. A number of warships can also be obtained in kit form.

The advantage of kits is that virtually all the armament and superstructure is included, often ready to fit and sometimes semi-finished. Nonetheless armament is something apart and consists mainly of guns from the heaviest down to machine guns.

The main armament is usually in turrets from which (depending on the type of ship) two or three barrels of a specific calibre protrude.

Some ships from World War II even had four guns per turret. Turrets differ according to the country of origin, the British differing completely from the German both in construction and appearance.

Gun barrels have a specific shape and if one is going to make them from a working drawing one should bear in mind that they are not simple tubes but are highly profiled. The barrels are made of wood or brass tube and with some scales the use of tubes fitting one within the other will not be very noticeable. The turrets can be made of wood or metal. Where the guns are actually required to shoot, the barrel must, of course be hollow. To give an idea of what a real gun was like some details are given of an English 15″ Naval gun.

The barrel itself was an example of craftsmanship of the highest order. They were over 16 m long and had an internal diameter of 38.1 cm in which grooves were turned along the length of the barrel. They comprised four tubes one within the other, the innermost having the lands and grooves. Around this was the second tube which had no less than 13 different diameters along its length. The third tube was about two-thirds the length of the first two and fitted precisely around them. The rest of the length was covered with closely wound layers of steel wire with a total length of 256 km (!). All this was surrounded by a further tube which was fitted with collars by which the barrel was supported and retained in the turret. Not so strange that such a barrel weighed 100 tons. Some idea of the measurements can be gained from Fig. 8.52.
The turrets on a ship are usually coded. Forward are A (the first) and B, and aft X and Y, X being in front. The anti-aircraft batteries amidships carry the letters P and Q.

8.54. An MTB with four single torpedo tubes.

When the gun was fired with a full charge a pressure of 3,200 kg/cm² was created in the firing chamber. The shell weighed about 860 kg and with the full charge of 225 kg cordite, was

8.55. Secondary armament of the American warship U.S.S. Missouri (Photo. U.S. Navy).

8.56. On a warship one can never have too much detail (Nürnberg, the author).

fired a good 25 km. Sometimes a smaller charge was used. The barrel could stand more than 350 full charge firings before the inner (or entire) barrel was replaced. The muzzle velocity of the shell was 200 m/sec. The thickening at the end of the barrel was strengthening against the enormous pressure wave behind the shell.

The turrets in a model can be made to rotate on a central axis and can be connected below decks to a servo or an electric motor with reduction gear. One can then turn them at command.

Torpedo tubes

On destroyers, torpedo boats and light cruisers one finds torpedo launching installations (rotatable through 360°). These usually comprise 4 or 5 torpedo tubes combined to fire in the same direction. Single tubes can be found on some motor torpedo boats. The firing installation is at the rear of the tubes. The torpedo, a slim bomb that travels at high speed (under water), fits precisely in such a tube. In reality the torpedos were fired toward the target by means of cordite or compressed air.

Wooden rod can be used to model torpedo tubes or one can use brass tube and/or plastic. Most models have static installations that are made to scale, but with some larger models the builders have even made installations capable of firing torpedos. We will return to this in Chapter 9. While access to supplementary information is handy when modelling merchant ships, it is vital to the modelling of warships.

9 Special functions

In model ships one can make an incredible number of operational functions. It is not our intention here to give a detailed description of how such functions can be incorporated, but rather to give the basic ideas from which the model builder can find his own way. One should try to maintain scale but in some instances one will have to make a compromise between functioning and scale.

We will go into somewhat more detail concerning sailing ships because we can work there from fundamental principles.

With scale models virtually everything can be made to operate (where necessary). It will be clear that this is easier with larger models than with small; a certain amount of space is essential for the drive mechanisms.

Bow thrusters

Many ships (ferry boats, sea-going tugs, offshore vessels) are equipped with bow thrusters. A bow thruster comprises a propeller with drive shafts mounted in a tube athwart the bow of the ship.

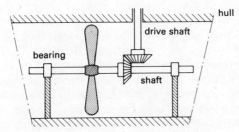
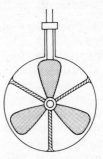

9.1.   How to build in a bow thruster.

The gearwheels must be small with respect to the diameter of the bow tube, otherwise they will present too great a resistance to the stream of water through the tube. One can use gears from toys or from kWh meters, preferably of plastic (or even brass). The tube for the drive shaft must extend above the water-line otherwise water will enter the boat. A nylon tube can be used as bearing at both ends of the shaft.

Fine gauze can be used to prevent weeds and other foreign matter entering the thruster tube. This can be cemented to the hull with epoxy cement but one must do it during the construction of the hull; one cannot get to it later. The motor for the bow thruster can be controlled either by a servo with reversing switch or by a separate speed control.

Anchor winch

One can have an anchor and chain on the forepeak as decoration but one can also make them work. In which case we need an anchor winch, which doesn't have to be to scale because we can mount it below decks. The winch comprises a drum (without axial movement) and a motor that can move axially along a sledge. On the drum one fixes a rectangular plate and on the motor a two-pronged fork that can grip the plate (Fig. 9.2). The motor needs a reduction gear of at least 1:150, and the anchor needs to be massive enough to run off the drum under its own weight. The drum should also run very light on its bearings. The chain should pass through an opening in the deck to wind round the drum and should be just as long as there is room on the drum.

The operation is simple: the motor is moved forward and backward by a linear servo. A switch is mounted such that the motor starts once the fork has engaged the drum. The motor then drives the drum so that the anchor is weighed. (Fig. 9.2 A). If the motor is withdrawn along its sledge a little it will be switched off, but due to the reduction gear the weight of the anchor is not enough to allow it to fall. If the motor is now further withdrawn along its sledge the fork will cease to engage the drum and the anchor will be dropped under its own weight. This is but an example; other systems will also come to mind.

180

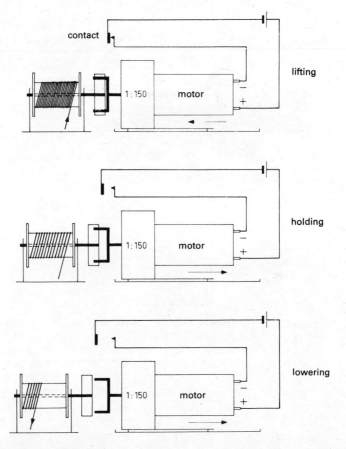

contact

lifting

1 : 150   motor

holding

1 : 150   motor

lowering

1 : 150   motor

9.2.   An effective winch.

Radar antennae

Rotating antennae are simple to make. One needs simply to mount a motor below decks and to couple it through a low reduction gear and a flexible drive to the shaft of the antenna.

Funnels that smoke

The smoke generators that are used with model locomotives can also be used for funnels; there are, however, special

9.3. The Jason has on board a rotating antenna, an operating hydrant, a syren and full navigation lights.

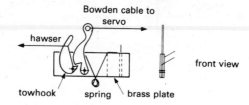

Bowden cable to servo

hawser

towhook   spring   brass plate

front view

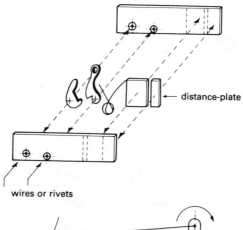

distance-plate

wires or rivets

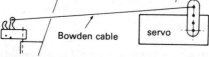

Bowden cable   servo

9.4.   A working tow hook.

smoke generators for ships. These are tubes that are closed at one end and which are fitted with an incandescent wire which can be connected to a 6 or 9 V supply. If the tube is filled with a special liquid the heat from the wire creates smoke.

Fog horn

For a fog horn one can resort to electronics and the many kits that can be bought. One can buy ready-to-use horns but don't consider a car horn – they are real current guzzlers.

Hoists and cranes

One can make hoists that actually work but it is far from simple with small scales. Something one will not be able to avoid is the use of genuine blocks. With a simple hoist one can make use of the same principles as the anchor winch. In this case the motor doesn't need to be mounted on a sledge but can be operated by a servo on which a switch is mounted. The same goes for cranes.

A tow hook that functions

The metal towing hook comprises the hook itself, a pawl, bowden cable, springs, and the servo that controls it. The pawl holds the towing hook in position. Once it is withdrawn via the operation of the servo, the hook turns and the rope falls off; the tug is thereby disconnected from its tow.

Water hydrants

The nozzles (fashioned in accordance with the drawing) are fitted on deck. The nozzle should be hollow and can be made of bronze tube that one shapes to fit the purpose. The jet with its base can be fitted to a disc that is connected below decks to a servo or a motor with a low reduction gear. The opening in the deck must be large enough to allow the hose to turn with the hydrant (the disc will ensure that the opening is out of sight). The other end of the hose must be connected to a

9.5. The Moorcock, too, has a radio-controlled towing hook.

pump – either an aquarium pump or the sort that one can buy in the model shops. A loose pump will have to be coupled to an electric motor. The pump must be fitted below the water and with an inlet that is a water-tight fit in the hull; it is better to use clamps on the hose to prevent it leaking or slipping off in use.

With a powerful motor one will get a respectable water jet and if one uses a speed regulator one will be able to adjust the reach of the jet which, together with the rotating hydrant will give a very realistic effect.

Lowering the boats

With some kits, such as the Adolph Bermpohl lifeboat, one finds instructions for lowering the boats. Should one prefer to

9.6. A detail of an East German fire tender. The hose on the reel (against the side railing), can be unrolled and connected to the hydrant.

use davits or a hoist one can make use of the same principle as the anchor winch. The lowering and raising mechanism will need to be equipped with blocks and tackle. Because both davits have to be operated it is better to fit an extra long drum (longer than the distance between the davits) coupled to a single winch motor. The rope from the left-hand davit is then wound on the left-hand end of the drum and that from the right-hand davit on the right-hand end. This way both davits will operate simultaneously and at the same speed. Naturally, a variable speed drive can also be used here.

Laying smoke screens

Warships are particularly suited to the addition of operating functions, one being smoke generators for smoke screens. Use is made of a powder (the same that fire-brigades use in exercises) which comes packed in cardboard tubes. The same sort of powder is also used to test airconditioning systems. A disadvantage of the stuff is the high temperatures needed and the fact that it leaves a dirty residue behind. For which reason it is rarely used with handsome scale models but more with specific classes in sailing demonstrations. The smoke powder is put in a metal container fitted with an incandescent filament.

Such filaments are used for a lot of purposes in model warships. One can use a glow-plug from an internal combustion motor but these are a little expensive for the purpose. It is cheaper to strip a short length of stranded wire, say about 10 cm, and wind a filament from a single strand. The ends

9.7. Laying a smoke curtain round one's own ship in order to hide it from the enemy (European Championships 1975 GB).

must be soldered to a pair of pins (isolated from each other) to which the supply can be connected. One will have to experiment a bit to obtain the best results, alter the length, perhaps, or use two strands instead of one. The type of charge one wishes to ignite will to a large extent determine how one fits the filament in the charge.

Guns that rotate and fire

To make the guns rotate one fits them to a pair of tubes so that one can rotate within the other, and couples them to a servo or an electric motor with a low reduction gear.

If required to fire, the barrels will have to be of bronze tube, to the rear end of which one has fitted an ignition coil, as described above, or a glow-plug. In the barrel one fits small sections of firework (those from a jumping cracker are suitable), the touch-paper of which is in contact with the ignition coil. The filament can be connected to a programmed servo so that as contact is made it becomes incandescent and the gun is fired.

Firing rockets

Around Guy Fawkes day fireworks are readily available in the shops and it is worth buying a few extra small rockets and instead of letting them off by the bonfire, saving them for your model boat. A mounting will be necessary which can be either

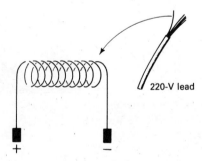

220-V lead

+   −

9.8.   Filament for igniting gunpowder.

186

a tube in which the rocket fits and from which it can be fired, or a pair of launching rails. Just as with the guns one can use a filament wherein the touch-paper of the rocket is pushed. One operates the servo and the rocket is launched.

Always take care that the ship is so positioned that people in the vicinity are not endangered. Your own and other people's safety is of prime importance. It can happen that damp prevents the rocket from firing in which case fit a new rocket and so dispose of the damp one that children are not tempted to experiment with it.

Other explosives

Any number of variations are possible: depth charges, air torpedos, quick-fire cannons, etc. Care is , however, essential in the use of fireworks. It is easy to injure other people or to damage their boats and in some countries a licence is required to let off fireworks. Will your insurance cover any damages?

9.9. The guns of the Nürnberg fire by means of fireworks and filaments in the barrels.

9.10. These machine guns on the Vosper MTB fire electronically (acoustically). Lamps on the muzzles simulate the flash.

9.11. A French patrol
boat sinks an enemy
ship with rockets.
(E.C., 1975, GB).

There is, of course, nothing against the occasional firework, but if one is going to make extensive use of them one needs to be very cautious. Learn as much about them as you can, work carefully and accurately. If one just wants the sound then one can do that by electronic means and with none of the risks.

Firing torpedos

In this case the word firing is a bit misleading. The torpedos are usually of (hard)wood and fit precisely in the torpedo tube, from which they are fired with the aid of a powerful spring. The spring needs to be firmly anchored in the end of the tube. On the underside of the tube a pawl is mounted which can be operated by a servo. The upper end of the pawl engages in a notch in the torpedo. When the servo is operated the pawl is withdrawn and the torpedo is fired out of the tube. It is easy to make the torpedos capable of floating so that they are recoverable. Some torpedos are fitted with a miniature electric motor and battery, whereby they can continue travelling for some metres. One will have to make such torpedos oneself and it is something one can only do if the scale of the model is not too small.

From the above you will have seen some of the special functions that can be fitted to model ships. The possibilities are actually numberless. At the European Championship at Welwyn Garden City in 1975, the Italians turned up with a com-

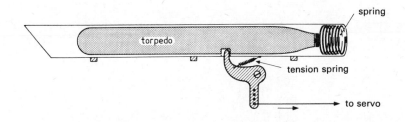

spring

torpedo

tension spring

to servo

9.12. Principle of a mechanical (model) torpedo launching installation.

plete D-day operation. They had aircraft carriers from which aircraft were catapulted. Cruisers and battleships were set on fire and sunk. Five submarines torpedoed landing ships. Landing ships that reached the shore opened their doors and amphibious vehicles and tanks emerged and with guns firing ascended the beach. Lifeboats were lowered from sinking ships; the lifeboats contained five rowers and with oars actually moving, 'rowed' 20 metres to the shore.

It is not surprising that many people wonder where it will all lead to. And what does that sort of thing cost in time and money?

Most model builders don't go to these lengths – it is, after all, a hobby. Nonetheless extra pleasure is obtained from a model that can do more than sail and steer. The boat becomes active and more nearly simulates the real thing.

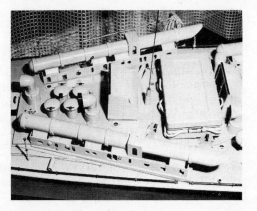

9.13. These torpedo tubes can fire (wooden) torpedos (A. Bedet, NL).

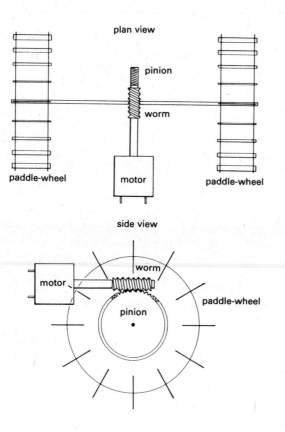

plan view

pinion

worm

paddle-wheel

motor

paddle-wheel

side view

motor

worm

paddle-wheel

pinion

9.14. Schematic suggestion for a paddle steamer drive.

Unusual ships

Paddle steamers

Paddle steamers can be propelled in various ways of which the most usual is paddle-wheels on both sides of the ship, about midships. The paddles are usually driven by a worm and gear system (Fig. 9.14). There are also models, such as the old Mississippi paddle steamers, that are propelled by a stern paddle. These can be belt driven.

A much better effect can be obtained if an electric motor with reduction gear is fitted below decks. The reduction can be a worm and wheel. If cranks are fitted to both sides of the wheel

9.15. An old Mississippi paddle steamer is very nostalgic. (M.S.V. Schwelm, BRD).

9.16 Pusher tugs (the one shown here is driven by a normal propeller) are not an everyday sight at a competition.

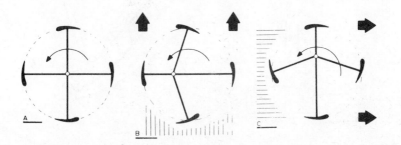

9.17. Principle of the Voith-Schneider propeller.

the motion can be transmitted to cranks on the paddle wheel via connecting rods. The cranks should be set at 90° to each other to avoid dead spots in the motion.

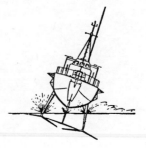

9.18.   An idea of a hydrofoil craft.

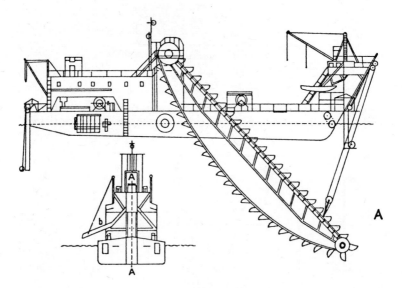

9.19.   A bucket dredger, unpowered but with a number of other functions.

Thrust boats

Another speciality is the building of a thrust boat. Even scale thrusters can be built. Some such boats are propelled by an unusual system – the so-named Voith Schneider propeller, which combines the functions of propeller and rudder.

In principle it comprises a horizontal disc to the underside of which are fitted a wreath of perpendicular aerofoils. These aerofoils alter position during each revolution so that their angle of attack varies as the disc revolves. The angle of attack changes from a positive value to zero and then to a negative. The direction in which the angle is zero can be altered at will, as can the value of maximum angle. This enables a thrust to be developed in any chosen direction and of any strength without changing the speed at which the disc rotates. Several models of this type are in operation in W. Germany.

9.20. A self-designed and self-built hovercraft. It steers fairly well.

Hydrofoil boats

Another boat with unusual properties is the hydrofoil boat. One needs an internal combustion engine to get the boat up out of the water and on its hydrofoils. It is certainly no easy boat to build.

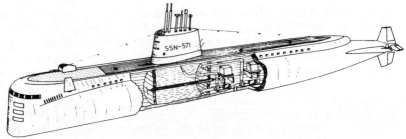

9.21. The height of specialisation is a working submarine.

9.22. A radio controlled decoy duck.

Dredgers

Another interesting speciality is the construction of bucket dredgers and the like. Working models are a joy to behold although one doesn't come across them often. Whether or not a dredger is fitted with its own propulsion system depends on the original one chooses as prototype.

194

Hovercraft

Many model builders have specialised in hovercraft and one can even obtain drawings from Model and Allied Publications (MAP). Internal combustion engines are used for propulsion usually with separate engines for propulsion and lift.

Submarines

The height of specialisation is the construction of model submarines. One not only has to take account of weight and

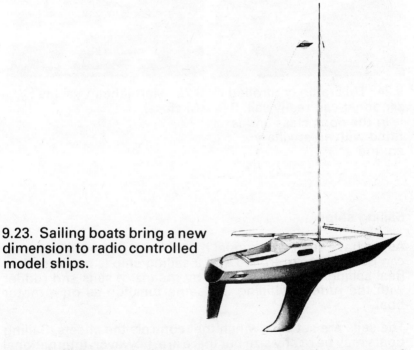

9.23. Sailing boats bring a new dimension to radio controlled model ships.

balance (filling and discharging ballast tanks) but also of pressure and the water-tightness of the hull. Some German, Italian and British model builders operate submarines. During the 1975 World Championship in England there was one Italian model builder who could not only completely manoeuvre his submarine under water, he could also fire Polaris missiles from it (also under water).

9.24. This radio controlled schooner can really sail. It is in the open class and is fitted with an auxiliary engine.

9.25. Marblehead yachts (M-class).

Sailing ships

As we have seen with model motor boats, virtually anything can be remote controlled and a sailing ship is no exception. Real sailing ships are steered by means of sails and rudder with the rudder fulfilling the same function as on a motor boat.

The sails are set by a winch that controls the sheets. Sailing boats may be of any size but there are, however, international classifications. The most common class is the M Class (Marblehead class) with a length of $50\frac{1}{4}$ ins maximum. Sail area is limited to 800 sq ins. Another class is the 10R (ten rater) and the rest fall either under the X or the K class. An exception is the large and heavy A class. The boats are usually rigged as is required by the regulations except, naturally for the X-class which is also known as the open class.

9.26. Competition sailing requires a good insight into the behaviour of ship and wind. (HMBC).

The exciting thing about sailing with radio controlled sailing ships is the interplay with the wind. That a boat can sail into the wind is the result of the billowing of the sail which thereby takes the form of an aerofoil. The wind passing over the sail generates 'lift' which operates on sail and boat. The forces can be split into two vectors, one which thrusts the boat forward and one which thrusts it sideways.

To prevent the boat drifting sideways one needs a large surface area, often increased by one or more heavy keels. Because one also needs to keep the ship as upright as possible (the higher the sail the more advantage one gains from the stonger wind which prevails some distance from the water) one tries to keep the centre of gravity as low as possible. Both reasons lead to a keel that is as deep as the depth of water will allow and which is ballasted as low as possible. This is fitted to a long narrow hull which offers the lowest resistance in the forward direction and the highest in the sideways direction. We now begin to get an idea of what the boat will look like. One can of course buy a boat but they are, however, expensive and one doesn't get the pleasure of building oneself. Those who are daunted by the thought of design and construction can buy one of the many kits that are available. They come complete, and anyone who is handy can make a fine X-class boat from one.

Kits are also available for M and 10R boats, plus a large selection of hulls only, mainly in polyester. If one's skill and

9.27. A glance inside an RC sailing boat. In the centre is the main winch for the sails, the rest is the receiver battery, the receiver and the rudder servo.

knowledge is insufficient one can usually get advice from a fellow model builder with more experience. One can, of course build an entire hull on the rib and plank system but this does demand a high degree of skill.

The overall construction of the boat depends in large measure on the height of the mast with respect to the length of the keel and its weight. A high mast (say 200 cm) has the advantage with low wind speeds, while with high wind speeds a shorter mast has the advantage. A light boat accelerates quickly but also falls off rapidly when the wind drops. In the last condition a heavier boat will continue ahead for a time but of course takes longer to come up to speed. There are innumerable variations with regard to size, weight, mast length, keel length and shape. The relationships one chooses depend on the purpose for which the boat is built. For a so-called touring boat one will choose a boat that is broad in the beam and has a fairly heavy keel. Such a boat can sail in all weathers and is very stable in the water. If one takes part in races it is as well to have a variety of sailing suits and keels so that the boat can be adapted to the prevailing weather.

There is sufficient room in the hull of a sailing boat to accommodate the radio control apparatus which the rules allow. One servo controls the rudder and, in place of a speed control one now has a winch to operate the sails. These proportionally controlled winches which allow the sheets to be slackened or taken up, as desired, can be obtained at the model shops. A sailing ship can be just as successfully sailed by radio control as a genuine yacht, and is a fast growing aspect of model boating.

10 The final touches

The model has now reached the point when it can be finished off. This will include varnishing or spraying, painting the waterline and the depth marks.

It is by these final details that a model ship stands or falls. There are any number of paints and lacquers available and one can use virtually any brand provided it is suitable for boats. Some models, such as sailing yachts and motor yachts, are finished in a high gloss. Passenger ships, freight ships and warships are finished either in eggshell or matt paint as are tugboats. The colour scheme will be found in the construction drawing and one should adhere to it if one wants a faithful representation of the ship being modelled.

Some paints refuse to dry on plastic, unless one uses the special plastic paints produced by Humbrol, Gloy or Revell.

10.1. A tugboat finished in high gloss paint lacks realism.

10.2. A model spray gun. It works on (canned) compressed air and can be used to spray small parts, often giving a better finish than a brush.

Model shops have an enormous variety of colours that are attuned to the colour schemes of model boats.

Wooden decks usually retain their wood colouring and are finished in clear or coloured varnish. Waterproof stain can also be used sometimes. Accessories or parts of metal and plastic can usually be sprayed to good effect. One can either use a normal spray gun or a spray-can, but one can also use one of the spray guns made specially for model boats (Fig. 10.2). Wood needs to be treated with pore-filler and/or primer. The instructions on the jar or tin will not only tell you how to handle the paint but also with what it should be thinned. When spraying, one should cover parts of another colour with adhesive tape.

Painting the water-line

Most ships are painted below the water line with a different colour than above it, often brick-red, black, green or brown. After several undercoats and having been sanded off as many times, the hull can be painted overall in the colour it will have above the waterline. When this has been thoroughly sanded a second top coat can be added and, if necessary a third.

When the paint is properly hard we determine the exact height of the waterline from the drawings. One needs a stable support for pencil or lining-in pen such as the home-built one

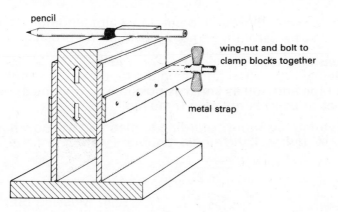

pencil

wing-nut and bolt to clamp blocks together

metal strap

10.3.   Jig for marking off the water line.

in Fig. 10.3. The hull should rest on a flat surface; if the keel gets in the way one may be able to turn the boat upside down. Care must be taken with the colour of pencil or ink used. The line must be visible while we work but not when the painting is finished.

Where the line is to be drawn one should go over the surface with an eraser which will make it matt enough to accept the pencil line. Don't press too hard on the eraser. Once the height of the pencil is correctly adjusted one can draw the line by moving it backwards and forwards along the hull. If this is properly done we will have a continuous line along the hull. One can now use transparent adhesive tape, vinyl insulating tape or plastic masking tape to mask off the paint above the line.

Never use crepe paper tape. Take care that the edge of the tape coincides exactly with the line with no air bubbles and with nice smooth curves. Sometimes, as with the sterns of tugboats, it is impossible to make a smooth curve with a single piece of tape, in which case after several layers of tape have been laid one above the other to approximate the final line we can use a sharp knife (draughtsman's knife) to carefully cut away to the exact line. Having got the tape right we can then paint the area below the line in its 'underwater' colour (after sanding, of course). It doesn't matter if paint gets on the tape, provided it doesn't go beyond it, and the border between tape and painted area must never be allowed to become a gutter filled with paint. Any paint tending to collect there must be carefully removed with a fine brush.

The masking tape should be removed before the paint is completely dry. When removing the tape keep the angle between tape and hull as small as possible so that the underlying coat of paint is not also removed.

If everything has gone according to plan you will now have a perfect waterline. If the model requires a waterline in the form

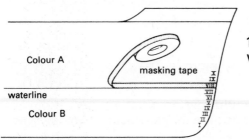

10.4. Masking off the waterline.

10.5.   Amidships of the Axel Johnson (N.Gerov, Bulgaria).

10.6.   Details on the fire tender of Wiegand (DDR).

10.7.   Note the Plimsoll line (A.Krowinkel, NL).

10.8.   A beautiful waterline (L.Drumec, Bulgaria).

of a thin stripe one now masks off again with two strips of tape and paints the stripe between (Figs. 10.5 to 10.8).

With some merchant ships the hull is painted in two colours (e.g. white with grey or with black) in which case one must mask off on a line below and parallel to the edge of the deck. Masking tape enables one to paint many different colours on one part.

10.9.   Various kinds of 'battleship grey'.

Other parts

The rest of the structure can be finished in the prescribed colours. Where necessary small parts can be painted separately. Some sections have to be painted during construction because they are either inaccessible or accessible only with difficulty at a later stage.

Deckhouses are usually white, although cream may be encountered with green decks. Hoists and masts are often yellow-ochre, but may also be of chrome yellow or light brown. Those parts of the mast above and behind the funnel are usually black with soot. Lifeboats often have covers which then makes the top grey, but if they are open the inside will be brown or wood coloured. Chains, just like the anchors, are a dull black with some brown rust stains, although very occasionally the anchors may be grey. Propellers are usually of bronze but sometimes have the grey tint of cast iron. The plastic propellers that one buys and which are usually red can be finished very handsomely in bronze.

With warships one must remember that not every grey is battleship grey. Every country, every period and every operational zone has had its own colour of grey, especially in the period between 1900 and 1945. One needs to be well aware of the zone and the circumstances in which a particular ship operated. During and after the first war the colour was generally a light grey, except in the tropics where white was used. Funnels and masts were yellow-ochre. German ships had a light grey superstructure with armament in the same colour while the hull was dark-grey. English ships on the other hand had a blue-grey colour (Admiralty grey) and the decks were, with a few exceptions, finished in dark green. The ships of other countries had decks of red-brown or black. During the war a good many changes took place.

Camouflage

In the time that radar was unknown or was in its infancy ships were often camouflaged. Because one was limited to visual observation one could try to trick one's enemy with regard to the recognition of silhouettes. The idea was that by painting the hull fancifully (sometimes with wooden dummies) one

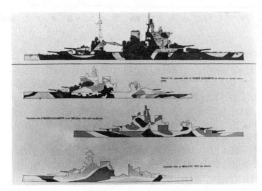

10.10.   Camouflage.

could create the impression that the enemy were confronted with an entirely different ship. Viewed from a distance camouflage completely changed the appearance of the ship.

With the growth of air reconnaissance and the development of radar during WWII, camouflage disappeared, although it lingered on in some areas until the end of the war. Ships of this period can, therefore, be camouflaged if desired.

The painting itself

However high the quality (and the price) of your paint you will never obtain a better finish than the surface on which you paint allows. Furthermore, one should paint somewhere where people are not always rushing to and fro and where there is as little soft furnishing as possible – the bathroom for example!

10.11. The Bismarck of T.Hamer (GB) in camouflage colours.

If one must paint somewhere else it must be somewhere where there is as little dust as possible in the atmosphere. No open doors or draughty windows and no-one galloping around. All the dust that is kicked up (whether you see it or not) will stick to newly painted surfaces. Where possible paint by daylight (by fluorescent lamp if necessary) and in any case by diffuse light so as to cut out hard shadows.

Paint individually as many parts as you can, and to keep them out of your way after painting hang them on a piece of string (before painting, of course).

10.12. Good brushes and well chosen paint give the best result.

10.13. Primed and sanded and now ready to be lacquered.

Use good quality brushes, cowhair being good and marten hair excellent, albeit expensive. The best place to buy them is at a shop supplying artists' necessities. Clean them after use in thinners or a brush cleanser. Brushes should be stored vertically with the brush upward or horizontally in a dust-free place. Try to build up a range of brushes including both flat and round. Before using a brush rub it on the palm of your hand in order to remove loose hairs, dust or specks of paint. One gets a smooth surface by sanding, for which one can use emery cloth, sandpaper and steel wool. Steel wool gives an exceptionally smooth finish and should be reserved for finishing. To sand off an undercoat one can use an ordinary cork holder for the flat surfaces and a strip of sandpaper round a wooden rod for the concave and convex surfaces. At the stationer's one can buy small emery boards (used to sharpen pencils) which are very handy for fine work. Having sanded off, all dust must be removed with a brush that is reserved (and marked) for the purpose. Of course, one doesn't sand off in the place where one paints. Do it preferably outside in order

10.14. The crew on deck are also painted.

to avoid 'troubles' in the family; actually this is a must with polyester, because in no time at all everything is white with dust.

Should one wish to give it another undercoat, and there can never be too many, one should first check the paint. This should be of such a viscosity that when a brush is dipped in and held about 30 cm above the tin, the paint flows off it in a thin continuous stream. If it is too thick it must be thinned but then with a little thinner at a time stirring well in between. Too much thinner means a spoiled pot of paint.

One should always use the thinner recommended by the manufacturer. Some paints can be thinned with turpentine (white spirits), for others we must use the correct thinner recommended. All types of thinner are inflammable, so don't forget the safety aspects while working. If the manufacturer has recommended a specific type of thinner then use it!

After the first undercoat one can still see the grain of the wood because the paint will have been absorbed by the wood. If pore-filler has been used this will, of course, be much less evident. Once the coat is dry one can sand again and, if necessary fill. Some fillers shrink which means that holes will have to be filled several times. This is less of a problem with two component filler, which furthermore, hardens off in about half an hour which makes for fast working. Normal fillers require 12 to 24 hours to harden sufficiently for sanding. Curved surfaces can best be filled using a filler sponge which follows the contours of the hull. A filling knife is much too stiff.

Very small areas can be filled using a razor blade. After sanding one must check the smoothness of the surface. If not, one must fill again. A good way of checking the surface is to paint it with a thin coat of paint which one then sands away after it has dried. Where paint remains one has a hollow that still needs further filling. Once this has been done one can give it a final undercoat.

This last coat is the one on which the first top-coat will come. Its smoothness should be checked when lighted from the side. At least two top-coats are needed and both must be of the correct thickness. The surface will no longer absorb paint, so what is brushed on stays on, which means a very thin coat of paint.

Spraying is, of course, better but demands some skill so one should spray a few test pieces before trying it on the boat. The first coat should be a very thin one and it is better to put on several coats than to try to do everything in one go. After use clean the sprayer properly and finally spray some thinners through it. Naturally one must mask off those parts that don't need to be painted in the colour one is using. Where possible one should use paints of the same brand; they are matched to each other and one doesn't get any unpleasant surprises.

To keep the paint as clean as possible one should transfer to another pot just as much paint as one expects to use in one session and thin it as necessary. After painting one throws pot and all away unless it is essential that the pot be used again, in which case empty it and clean it with thinners before using it again. In either case we have got rid of all the dust and suchlike that has collected in the paint.

When the first top coat is thoroughly hard one can consider finishing it off with steel wool (No. 400 wet and dry is also good). The surface should then be cleaned off with a damp cloth. When the surface is dry one can begin with the following top coat. Naturally, if one wants to add a third top coat one will have to smooth off before doing so.

Metal parts must first be treated with primer, then with undercoat of appropriate colour and finally with a single top coat.

One last piece of advice. Everytime you paint, fill or sand your ship do the same with a reasonably sized piece of the same material. If you leave a little of the previous coat visible with each new coat you paint on you have a check on how many coats you have laid on and you also have a place where you can check as to whether the paint is hard or not without putting your fingers on your ship.

Depth marks.

A point that is often forgotten in the construction of model ships is the depth marks of which the most common and most important is the Plimsoll line. This must be on both sides of the ship amidships as shown in Fig. 10.15 (but without the figures which are simply shown for illustration).

This line derives its name from a certain Samuel Plimsoll, but the honour should really go to James Hall who was director of a shipping concern and an expert for Lloyds shipping insurance. It was obvious at that time that shipping losses due to overloading were so common that legal action was necessary. No maritime law is complete without some definition as to maximum load. Nonetheless it took 16 years before the law was amended on this point, and because Lloyds is the most important maritime insurer in the world the law became very quickly internationally applied.

The strength and construction of the ship determines at what distance below the deck the line of maximum loading is drawn. This distance is known as the minimum freeboard (the horizontal line within a circle).

If one looks at the complete depth line one will see that it is dependent on the time of year and the salt content of the water, (on its specific gravity, therefore). A stated cargo tonnage refers always to the summer line in seawater.

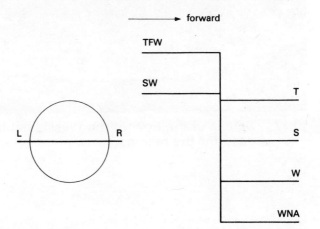

10.15. The Plimsoll line. TFW = tropical fresh water, SW = tropical sea water, S = summer depth in sea water, W = winter depth in sea water and WNA = winter depth in North Atlantic waters.

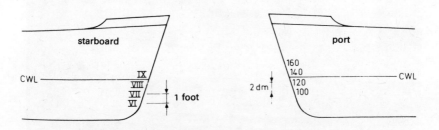

10.16. One also finds depth marks on both sides of the bow.

10.17. Details of the bow of the Wesselina. Insect gauze is used for the railings.

10.18. The Wesselina again, but here aft.

Apart from the Plimsoll line there are also other lines on both sides of the ship at bow and stern. These lines show if the ship is evenly loaded and show its absolute depth in the water. (Fig. 10.16).

On the starboard side the symbols are in Roman figures and on the port side in arabic figures. The deck line is at the height of the deck. The distance between the figures is 20 cm on the port side and 1 foot (30.48 cm) on the starboard side (in real ships, of course).

One can paint the symbols on or one can make use of transfers or stickers, in which case a coat of clear lacquer is essential to make them water resistant.

11   Radio Control

In previous chapters we have mentioned some of the building blocks that go to make up a radio control system. We have mentioned, thereby, that such parts as servos, receiver and speed control must have a definite place in the hull and must be correctly mounted.

Servos can be held in place by spring clips which are screwed to the hull. When pushed between the springs the servo will be firmly held in place. Another method is to screw the servo in a frame of wood or metal, the brackets on the servo mount then being fitted with rubber bushes to absorb vibration (Fig.

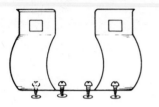

11.1. Spring clips for the servo (Microprop).

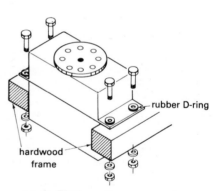

rubber D-ring

hardwood frame

11.2. Fitting the servo in a wooden frame.

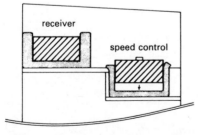

receiver

speed control

11.3.   Bedded in foam plastic.

11.1 and 11.2). Spring clips are also usually fitted with shock absorbing rubber rings.

The receiver, speed control and, if necessary the battery, can be bedded in foam rubber or plastic. The other parts can now be connected to the receiver. Connection must be made to agree with the joystick positions chosen. For example, if one has decided that the left-hand joystick will control the speed, then the speed control must be connected to that output of the receiver that is controlled by the left-hand joystick.

The transmitter

The transmitter comprises a closed metal or plastic box which contains the requisite electronics and the battery. On the top or the front of the transmitter one finds: an antenna; (usually) a meter; one or two joysticks; trim controls; a battery charger socket; and, naturally a main switch. We will take each item individually:

11.4. A 3-channel transmitter.

11.5.   A simple radio control is easy to install, as shown here on the Cutter 'Gina'.

The *antenna* transmits the high frequency signal produced by the transmitter. The antenna is telescopic and when pulled right out operates at its highest strength; the more it is pushed in the weaker the signal it transmits. The antenna may be removable.

From the *meter* one can see whether the transmitter is switched on or not; when switched on the pointer is displaced. The scale is divided into zones, for example, red, black and green, reading from left to right. These zones indicate the condition of the battery and thereby the operational state of the transmitter. With the pointer in the green zone the battery is fully charged. After a time it will drop back to the black zone and when the battery is discharged will come to rest in the red zone. The battery must now be charged up as the transmitter is not in a state to operate reliably.

Some *joysticks* are so constructed that they can move in all directions, for example, forward and sideways simultaneously. With other types they can move only one direction

216

11.6. A
self-made
6-channel
transmitter
with (left)
several servos.

at a time, say, right or left (in a slot) or forward and backward.
Some are sprung so that they always return to neutral when
released. The joysticks are usually used to control the main
functions of the ship, the right hand for steering to left or right
and the left hand for the speed control plus ahead or astern. A
good radio control system gives one as much control of the
ship as if one stood on board at the wheel.

The *trim controls* enable one to adjust the neutral position of
the related joystick and thus the on-board servo.

Apart from the trim controls one may encounter other *drive
controls*. These control the auxiliary functions. The number of
channels a radio control system has determines the number
of functions that can be directly controlled by the system.

With one channel one can move one servo from its neutral
position to either left or right. One can therefore connect one
servo to each channel, four servos to a four channel system,
for example, in which, for simplicity, the speed control is
treated as a servo.

Some manufacturers create confusion by calling a six channel system a twelve channel one. In doing so, they count both
positions of each servo as separate channels, which is non-
sense. All positions of a servo arise from a single movement
although we can certainly control various functions (e.g.
switches) by a single servo.

Most transmitters have also a connection for *charging,* usually a DIN socket.

The *main switch* is used to switch the transmitter on or off. If the antenna is removable *never switch the transmitter on with the antenna removed — it will be the unheralded end of your transmitter.* Transmitters operate at specific frequencies, which are determined by a quartz crystal plugged somewhere into the transmitter. With some transmitters the crystal with its base is mounted on the outside of the case so that if one needs to change frequencies it is easy to change crystals. The manufacturer (and the GPO) determine which crystals can be mounted in transmitter and receiver (because that has a crystal, too).

Frequencies and operation

The term frequency has already been used but without any indication as to its actual meaning. The world about us is filled with vibrations (waves). Some we can hear (sound), some feel (warmth) and some see (light). But that isn't the end of the story; consider UV radiation and X-rays which we cannot normally observe but which are very important to our lives. And to come closer to home, your radio receives its 'sound' via electro-magnetic vibrations. The subject is much too complex to discuss here, even briefly, but there are enough books on the subject if you are interested. In this context the important thing is how radio commands can be conveyed via vibrations.

The number of vibrations per second is known as the frequency and is expressed in Hertz (in some publications, cycles per second). Audible sound is usually described by tone and light by colour, but those frequencies that we cannot observe we express in Hertz.

The (young) human ear responds to sound up to about 20 000 Hz. As we get older this drops to about 10 000 Hz. Dogs can hear much higher tones which is why some dog whistles emit a tone that is too high for the human ear, but to which a (well trained) dog will respond.

Coming back to our subject: the frequency (the carrier wave) of your radio control is also expressed in Hertz, usually around 27 000 000 Hz. To avoid so many zero's use is made of decimal prefixes. 20 000 Hz = 20 kHz (kilohertz) and 27 000 000

Hz = 27 MHz (megahertz). Both transmitter and receiver are tuned to a very narrow frequency band by their crystals, how narrow depends on the 'selectivity'.

Should a transmitter operate at a frequency of 27.145 MHz, then the receiver should only react to that frequency. In practice it will react to frequencies between about 27.143 and 27.147 MHz, depending on the selectivity of the receiver. If it is less selective it will cover a broader frequency band and the chance arises that it will react to commands on an adjacent channel.

The selectivity of your receiver determines, in important measure, whether you can operate your ship in the vicinity of other enthusiasts. If your receiver is sufficiently selective and you operate at the right frequency you can operate at the same time as someone else. At least, provided you both operate on different frequencies.

In order to indicate on which frequency one is operating one hangs a coloured pennant from the antenna. So if you see someone operating with an orange pennant on his antenna and you operate also on the orange band, forget it! Both receivers would react to both transmitters – and that would mean disaster. It is to prevent such calamities, and the consequent disagreements, that most clubs operate a system whereby one can see at a glance which frequencies are in use. Sometimes it is a pole on which the frequencies in use are indicated by clothes pegs in the appropriate colour. Sometimes it is a board where similar pegs indicate the frequencies. One checks first on the board to see if one's colour is still

11.7. Transmitting on the proper frequency. The pennant indicates the colour code.

there (the board shows the unused frequencies), removes it and clips it on the antenna. If you use interchangeable crystals and the 'orange' is gone but the 'green' is still available, then one plugs in the green crystal *not forgetting to change the one in the receiver*.

The GPO has allocated specific frequency bands to model radio control. Within these bands we distinguish channels that can be used independently of each other.

Channel	Frequency (MHz)	Colour
4	26.995	brown
9	27.045	red
14	27.095	orange
19	27.145	yellow
24	27.195	green
30	27.255	blue

It is forbidden to transmit on other frequencies and some countries operate on different frequencies so it is as well to check this point when taking part in international events abroad. The tolerance on the frequency is limited to only 1.5 kHz. On channel 14, therefore, the limit is 27.095 − 0.0015 = 27.0935 and 27.095 + 0.0015 = 27.0965 MHz!

Digital/proportional

In brief, a digital system works only on impulses. The transmitter, therefore, doesn't work on tones but on impulses created by interrupting the carrier wave at specific intervals. Virtually all radio control systems operate on the digital principle. There are, however, many variations in the type of radio control one can buy. These variations involve differences in construction and partitioning, in design and functioning as well as the way in which the receiver processes the information it receives.

The term proportional speaks for itself: the servos operate in the same measure as the control is moved. Move the joystick halfway and the servo will move halfway.

The main control functions of both joysticks are transmitted to the servos via specific outputs from the receiver. Which is why one must first ascertain if the right hand joystick for example, really does operate the rudder. The left-hand will then operate the accelerator or the speed control. One can indicate the functions on a transmitter with name tabs. (Fig. 11.8).

The apparatus shown is a 6-channel transmitter with removable antenna. The right-hand joystick has two positions: ahead and astern. The left-hand can only move to right and left. Directly beneath them (in the dark area) are two trimmers and 4 proportional controls for auxiliary functions.

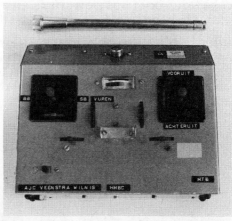

11.8. A 6-channel digital transmitter.

In the centre is a bracket to which one can fit a carrier strap by means of clips, which leaves both hands free for control. No special knowledge is needed to operate a radio system. The equipment available through the trade is of high quality, meets the highest standards and requires virtually no maintenance.

12 Sailing, individually and with a club

If the autumn and winter are the times for construction it is the spring and summer that are the seasons for sailing; pleasure, thus, the whole year through. With a motor driven boat one can sail virtually everywhere, but membership of a club has definite advantages, and can be interesting as well as instructive.

Model boats have an almost magnetic influence on the general public, as you will soon discover once you try sailing a boat. One sets the model in the water, by which we mean suitable water: a pond or suchlike, with no shipping or high waves, no strong currents and free of water plants or weed. Plants tend to get entangled in the propeller and can lead to a burnt out motor unless proper fusing has been fitted. In any case your boat lies powerless and out of reach, so no water plants!

After putting the boat in the water one must check the balance; it mustn't list to one side. It should also sink fully to the waterline. Any lead weights used to balance the ship should finally be cemented in place. If the ship has a removable antenna don't forget to fit it in place.

12.1. Sailing alone.

12.2. Sail as naturally as possible.

One should try to operate the ship as steadily and naturally as possible and sometimes this demands a bit of practice, certainly when the ship is sailing towards you. If the command is given to turn to starboard, the joystick will have to be moved to the right. From where you are standing the ship moves to the left and with the control to port it moves to the right. It's best if you can think yourself into a position behind the wheel of the boat when everything will fall into place. This is certainly true in emergencies when you must act fast and accurately. When a neighbouring boat is bearing down on yours you must do the right thing, first time, to avoid a collision.

Always keep your model in sight; if it is too far away you cannot judge if it is answering properly; if it has run into weed or has been holed, nor do you know if the batteries for reception and sailing have sufficient charge. You can now also check the power of your transmitter. Assuming that the batteries are well charged – calculation will tell how long you can operate, one starts with the antenna telescope right in. In this condition the antenna transmits the weakest possible signal, just enough to control a model that is close by.

After the ship has sailed some metres it will cease to answer the helm, so one extends the antenna until it is under control again. So doing you can judge the optimal reception and by remembering where the ship was each time it became uncontrollable can gain a good idea of your limits. It is impossible to state a fixed distance but if your ship is still under control with antenna in at a distance of 100 metres one should not try to improve it. The maximum has been reached. Apart from attaining a natural style in sailing one should also try to learn how to lay alongside properly. It requires some practice but is

12.3. Berthing is very difficult, certainly with waves such as these.

well worth while, and will be necessary if you go in for competition sailing. Even if one does not it is a pleasure to master the art of berthing your boat in as genuine a manner as possible. It is easier with a speed control but can also be done with a step control.

When berthing one will have to allow for the rotation of the screw. With a propeller that turns anti-clockwise it is best to approach the berth from the left, that is, with the starboard to the quay. With a propeller that turns clockwise one can best approach from the right with the port-side to the quay. When berthed the ship should lie parallel to the quay and at the minimum distance from it, and the manoeuvre should be so executed that the ship lies still at the requisite place.

One can begin the manoeuvre by approaching the quay at a certain angle depending on the size and manoeuvrability of the ship. If the ship has a propeller that rotates anti-clockwise and a speed control, one sets the speed control at slow ahead and stops the motors when the ship is about 1 m from the side. During competitions it is best to come in in a large curve.

If one wants to lie alongside from the left (starboard) one should give the ship a little port rudder. This will turn the ship to port, and to reduce speed one lets the motors run astern. The anti-clockwise rotating screw will now pull the stern to starboard thus increasing the turn to port. Using propulsion and rudder the steersman should so execute the manoeuvre that the ship comes to lie still parallel to the quay.

With a clockwise rotating propeller one performs the manoeuvre in the same way but mirror-imaged. One should also allow for the direction of rotation of the propeller when going astern.

With double-screwed ships (where the sideways forces of the propellers cancel each other), one gains no advantage when berthing unless the speeds of the propellers are individually controlled. A bow thruster also simplifies berthing.

Unfortunately, among the dozens of interested watchers who have turned up in the meantime there are a number who not only need to look with their eyes, but also with their hands. So just check quickly to see that everything on deck is properly screwed down. It often costs evenings of work to make good the damage and the parts that disappeared via souvenir hunters. In this connection it is worth recommending that you keep an eye on all those things you have lying around on the bank, such as your toolbox, spare batteries, transmitters and possibly a second boat. It is difficult to keep an eye on everything and even more difficult to act if something is going amiss.

Clubs

Apart from sailing alone one can also join a club which offers undoubted advantages. One receives the club magazine with a lot of information of interest to the model boat builder, and on club evenings one can swap experiences with fellow model builders and gain advice and experience. The friendly atmosphere and the many film and slide evenings plus working and building weekends means that one can often build up in a short time a fund of knowledge that would otherwise take years of sailing alone. One becomes at home in the subject

12.4.   A club event (HMBC, The Hague).

and learns how to get on well with one's colleagues. Clubs usually have a range of literature (sometimes also foreign) about model boat building, which will enable you to gain information about the boat you are building.

During the official sailing season (from April to October) regular sailing events are held and both national and international competitions are organised. The clubs work together so that the important events are shared out fairly.

The organising club takes care of invitations and of railing or roping off the enclosure where the members and their boats can be secure. There are usually also tables, tents and a hired public address system, and if the bank is unsuitable, a temporary jetty or pontoon is provided, which allows the heaviest models to be easily launched.

12.5. A roped-off enclosure for a sailing event (HMBC, The Hague).

12.6. Starting point for scale models at Welwyn Garden City in England during the European Championships, 1975.

An entrance fee is usually required for competitions which is used to help defray the expenses.

During such events the models are usually on tables and although they are much safer in a railed off enclosure than when sailing alone, it is really essential that non-members are kept outside the enclosure. This is often difficult to do during important events: the members charged with keeping order can't be everywhere at once – and the public usually numbers hundreds!

It is important, too, that the organisers arrange for a suitable stretch of water and the necessary permission for sailing. One can't just set up tents and tables where one likes. They are usually very well organised and make a wonderful experience. If the weather is good there is usually a large interested public who not only share the experience with the competitors but also ask for explanations.

Sometimes a couple of members are chosen to represent the club at international events, where they not only learn a great deal but also make new friends. How far afield such members are sent tends to depend on the club's finances. And with return events, friendships are renewed and if everything has gone well the participants are richer in experience and the club in members.

Organisations and clubs

To conclude, ten commandments for participation in events and competitions. As a regular participator in such events (in The Netherlands) I hereby anticipate the sometimes unsporting behaviour of other participants.

The humorous tone disguises a number of truths that, unfortunately, turn out to be all too important in practice.

1. Arrive at least an hour too late.
2. Open your big mouth and demand an immediate turn at sailing.
3. At once take the greater part of your boat to pieces so that a lengthy delay results.
4. At the same time roundly curse the organisers, the members and the public.

5. Borrow tools but don't return them.
6. Remove the silencer from your internal combustion engine so that everyone knows that it is a sailing event.
7. Crowd everybody while setting your boat in the water and ensure that at least one transmitter belonging to someone else falls in the water.
8. Don't wait until your predecessor has lifted his boat out of the water but use your stonger transmitter to ensure that it smashes against the jetty.
9. Sail your boat for longer than is allowed.
10. Lift your boat from the water, kick someone else's ship into limbo and depart cursing for home.

And, finally, be amazed when the chairman tells you that you are no longer a member of the club;

Many clubs in Great Britain are members of the Model Power Boat Association and a list of clubs can be obtained from the General Secretary: G. Colbeck, 19 Lea Walk, Harpenden, Herts.

13 Competition classes, rules and circuits

For competitions and for national and international championships certain rules are necessary, rules which the participants must observe, and which create an equal chance for all. This is achieved by setting comparable ships in specific classes. This is regulated internationally by NAVIGA who are also responsible for laying down the rules.

Model ships are divided into 25 classes according to type, scale, size, propulsion and steering. The most important of these will be mentioned here, beginning with static models. The competition element with such ships is fidelity in copying the original. The models are judged by a knowledgeable jury who have photos and drawings of the original at their disposal. Their verdicts are given in the form of points, the average being the result obtained by the competitor. In arriving at their verdict the jury take account of the work involved in the model, the degree of difficulty, the scale, the construction and the painting.

Static models are in Class C:

C1 – models without motor, for example, sailing ships.
C2 – models with motor(s), for example, tugboats.

13.1. Waterline models are only judged on their fidelity. (John Brown & Co. Ltd., Glasgow, Scotland.).

13.2.   An EK class warship (A. Lagoutin, USSR).

C3 – models of harbour installations, for example, wharves, docks, and suchlike.
C4 – miniature models and dioramas to a scale of 1:250 or smaller.

Building in electric motors, combustion engines and steam engines (later with radio control) lead to the classes being extended and, in consequence, the rules.

For a number of model builders the construction remained the important thing. Although motors were built in to the model and the rudder operated, there was no radio control. The engine was started by hand and the rudder was manually set. In competition these models sail over a straight course, with the intention that the rudder is so adjusted that it passes through various pairs of buoys at the end of the course, thus earning a number of points. These models are in the 'E' Class:

EH merchant ships and pleasure yachts
EK warships
EX ships to own design – the open class.

With radio control one can sail a ship round a course marked off by buoys. This class, the F2 Class, is the most important for scale models. The course comprises a number of gates marked out by buoys; the boat must go astern through a similar gate and berth in a dock. If one does this faultlessly one earns the maximum of 100 points. Penalties are given for missing or

13.3. The competition course for the E class.

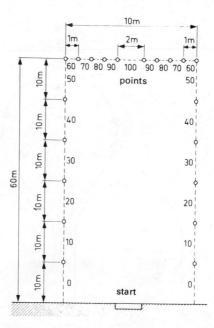

touching buoys, failing to sail properly astern, etc. Just as with static ships the construction itself is judged and here, too, a maximum of 100 points can be earned. The total number of points (construction + sailing) determines one's place in the final classification.

The F2 Class is subdivided into three:

F2A models with a length of 70 to 110 cm
F2B models with a length of 110 to 170 cm
F2C models with a length of 170 to 250 cm, and models to a scale greater than 1:100.

Theoretically, at least, the course itself will give little difficulty, berthing is, however, another matter. After passing through the final gate (astern) one must berth in a specially constructed 'dock'.

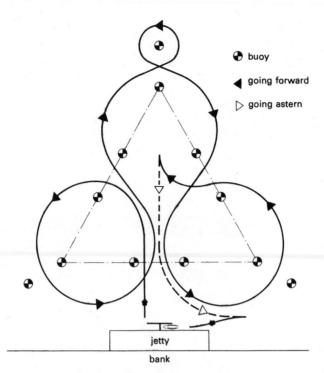

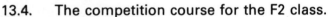

○ buoy

◀ going forward

▷ going astern

jetty

bank

13.4.   The competition course for the F2 class.

13.5. All the F2 class can be seen here: in the background is the sail team. (HMBC, The Hague, Photo: Stokvis).

232

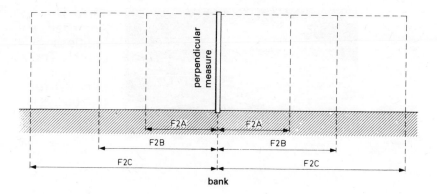

bank

13.6.   The measuring area for scale models.

a) One may enter the dock from left or right.
b) During the berthing operation a member of the jury will be present on the jetty.
c) Fig. 13.6 shows how the dock is marked off for the various classes. This area may only be entered once; it is not permitted to re-attempt the berthing operation once one has entered the measured off area.
d) The model should be so berthed that the bow lies within the area indicated for that class and with the boat parallel to the jetty (but without touching it). In this position the model should remain still for three seconds, during which time the transmitter may not be operated. The distance between ship and jetty should not be more than 15 cm.
e) The areas for the various classes are:
   F2A 40 × 30 cm,
   F2B 40 × 50 cm,
   F2C 40 × 80 cm,

   In each case, 40 cm is the length of the perpendicular measure.

10 points are awarded for a correct berthing manoeuvre. Contacting either the jetty or the perpendicular measure loses one 5 points. Contacting both or failing to enter the measured area costs one all 10 points.

13.7. The Aegir sails a faultless course. The distance between the two buoys is 100 cm.

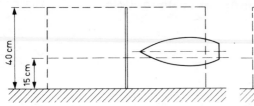

good = 10 points

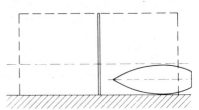

clear of jetty but
touching perpendicular measure = 5 points

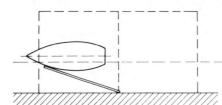

boat beyond measured-off
area = 0 points

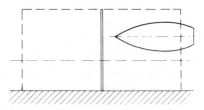

parallel to jetty but
touching it = 5 points

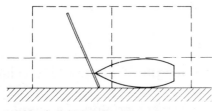

touching both jetty and
perpendicular measure = 0 points

bow within measured-off area
but too far from jetty = 5 points

13.8.   The points awarded for berthing.

13.9. Rehearsing for an F6 demonstration. For this show an hour's preparation is needed on-site (HMBC, The Hague).

13.10. F7 demonstration by the Admiral Scheer of Horst Muster which has 32 functions.

Teams

With boats that can do more than just sail and steer, i.e., that are equipped with special functions, there is a special class, the F7. Here one has 10 minutes to carry out a programme that has been previously presented to the jury. Any number of functions may be operated, and for the entire show one earns a number of points.

Even more interesting are the team events in which a number of members combine to perform a 'show'.

Within the 10 minutes allowed one can simulate a 'real' event, such as taking a sinking ship in tow; extinguishing a fire on a tanker or drilling platform; raising a sunken wreck and towing it to harbour, or mimicking a sea battle, etc. This class is the F6. Just as with the F7 one has to present one's programme to the jury beforehand.

Sail Classes

The course for radio controlled sailing ships is shown in Fig. 13.11. The triangle has sides of 50 to 60 m and the first leg is laid off into the wind. The starting line must be at least 10 m long and must be perpendicular to the first leg. A sketch of the course must be clearly displayed near the starting line.

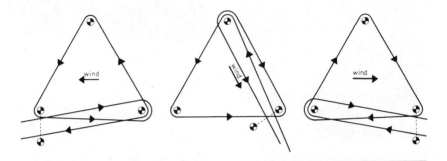

13.11. Several ways of laying out the sail course.

There are three classes:

F5M the Marblehead Class
F5-10 the Ten-Rater
F5X the open class (maximum 5,000 cm² sail area).

At the end of each race a list is made of the finishing order. Each place earns a number of points and the points earned in each heat are totalled for the final classification. The organisers may decide that lowest heat doesn't count toward the final classification. The starting signal may be given with wind speeds of between 1 to 10 m/s. Sails are measured before starting.

Each boat must be certified by the national association and receives a certificate of compliance and a national registration number that must be displayed on the sail with the class sign. There are extensive regulations for competition sailing with sailing boats which can be obtained from the Model Yacht Association.

Model speed boats

A lot of people like racing model speedboats, using for the purpose internal combustion engines which bring with them the problem of noise. There are national and international limits laid down but some local councils have even stricter regulations, so it is always worth enquiring beforehand what

236

the local regulations are. The Model Power Boat Association level is 80 dbA measured at a distance of 10 metres.

The coming of the nickel-cadmium cell has led to the introduction of electric motor powered speedboats which can attain the same speed as speedboats powered by internal combustion engines of 5 cc approx. It takes only a few minutes, however, to completely discharge the batteries.

The classes for speed boats are:

F1-E1   Speedboats with electric motor and a total weight of not more than 1 kg.

F1-E500 Speedboats with electric motor and of unlimited weight but with a maximum battery voltage of 42 V.

F1-V2.5 Speedboats with internal combustion engines of up to 2.5 cc capacity.

F1-V5   Speedboats with internal combustion engine of up to 5 cc capacity.

F1-V15   Speedboats with internal combustion engine of up to 15 cc capacity.

Also, in Great Britain, classes are recognised for electric models weighing a maximum of $2\frac{1}{2}$ kilogram, and internal combustion powered models for up to 35 cc engines, known as F1-E2.5 kg and F1-V35.

There are also two classes where speed is not the main consideration but the skill which one can lay off a given course.

13.12. Competition sailing is a fascinating branch of model ship construction.

13.13.   Registration marks on a radio controlled M class ship (dim. in mm).

13.14. In a competition one only has a few minutes to start the engine. If it fails to start within the allotted time the competitor has forfeited his chances before sailing the course. (HMBC, The Hague).

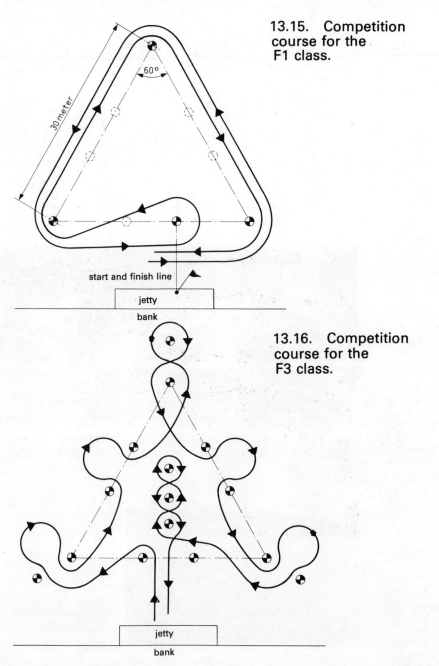

13.15. Competition course for the F1 class.

30 meter

60°

start and finish line

jetty

bank

13.16. Competition course for the F3 class.

jetty

bank

239

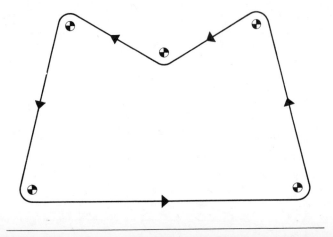

13.18. The FSR boat of M.Legué (NL), multiple Dutch champion and European champion in 1975 in the junior class.

13.19. An FSR race under way.

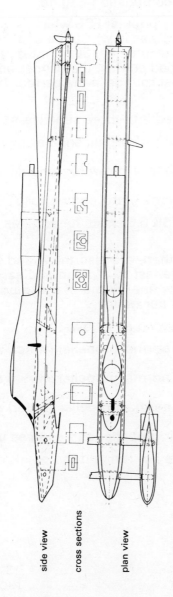

side view

cross sections

plan view

13.20. A construction plan for a hydroplane class A3: length 1,090 mm, breadth 220 mm, weight 1,000 g appr. With an OPS60 motor this boat can reach a speed of about 180 km/hr (designed by G.Mirov, Bulgaria.).

These are F3E for boats with an electric motor and F3V for boats with an internal combustion engine.

Another class is the very popular FSR which is for boats with internal combustion engines in which the endurance of man and boat are tested to the limit. For 30 minutes up to 12 boats race around an M-shaped course, the winner being the one who completes the most rounds in the period. The course is shown in Fig. 13.17.

This class is also divided into three sub-classes:

FSR $3\frac{1}{2}$ Speedboats with glowplug engine up to $3\frac{1}{2}$ cc capacity.

FSR15   Speedboats with a glowplug engine up to 15 cc capacity.

FSR 35   Speedboats with a petrol engine up to 35 cc capacity.

In Great Britain class FSR 6.5 exists for engines up to 6.5 cc capacity.

For some speedboats there are also the A and B classes in which the boat is made fast to a pylon and sails flat-out in circles on the end of its line. Some of these boats develop speeds of over 200 km per hour!

The classes are sub-divided as follows:

A1 Speed boats with a normal propeller (water) and engines up to $2\frac{1}{2}$ cc.

A2 Speed boats with a normal propeller (water) and engines up to 5 cc.

A3 Speedboats with a normal propeller (water) and engines from 5 – 10 cc.

B1 Speedboats with air propeller and engines up to $2\frac{1}{2}$ cc.

In these classes 5 heats are run and the points are totalled.

APPENDIX 1 **Various Tables**

Table 1 Battery Data

Make and type	No. of cells mA	Voltage V	Capacity mA.h	Max. current	Life (hours)
VARTA-DEAC Batteries					
100 DK	1	1,2	100	10	10
2/ 100 DK	2	2,4	100	10	11
3/ 100 DK	3	3,6	100	10	11
4/ 100 DK	4	4,8	100	10	12
5/ 100 DK	5	6	100	10	12
150 DK	1	1,2	150	10	14
2/ 150 DK	2	2,4	150	10	14
3/ 150 DK	3	3,6	150	10	15
4/ 150 DK	4	4,8	150	10	15
5/ 150 DK	5	6	150	10	15
225 DK	1	1,2	225	22	13
2/ 225 DK	2	2,4	225	22	14
3/ 225 DK	3	3,6	225	22	14
4/ 225 DK	4	4,8	225	22	14
5/ 225 DK	5	6	225	22	14
225 DKZ	1	1,2	225	22	13
2/ 225 DKZ	2	2,4	225	22	14
3/ 225 DKZ	3	3,6	225	22	14
4/ 225 DKZ	4	4,8	225	22	14
5/ 225 DKZ	5	6	225	22	15
451 D	1	1,2	450	50	12
500 DKZ	1	1,2	500	50	14
2/ 500 DKZ	2	1,2	500	50	14
3/ 500 DKZ	3	3,6	500	50	14
4/ 500 DKZ	4	4,8	500	50	14
5/ 500 DKZ	5	6	500	50	14
10/ 500 DKZ	10	12	500	50	14
2/1000 DKZ	2	2,4	1000	100	13
10/1000 DK	10	12	1000	100	15
Unit with 2 VARTA- DEAC 2/400 DK	2 × 2	2 × 2,4	400	50	11
Unit with 2 VARTA-DEAC 2/500 DKZ	2 × 2	2 × 2,4	500	50	15
Unit with 2 VARTA-DEAC 5/500 DKZ	2 × 5	2 × 6	500	50	15
VARTA-Lead Cells					
Wf3	1	2	3000	100	40
3 Wf 1	3	6	1000	100	14
3 Wf 3 k	3	6	3000	100	40
3 Wf 5 k	3	6	5000	500	16

Make and type	No. of cells mA	Voltage V	Capacity mA.h	Max. current	Life (hours)
SONNENSCHEIN 'dryfit' Batteries					
dryfit PC 1 Fx 5 S	1	2	7500	500	23
dryfit 2 Ax 2 F	2	4	900	100	12
dryfit PC 3 Ax 2 S	3	6	900	100	12
dryfit PC 3 Bx 3 S	3	6	1800	100	25
dryfit PC 3 Gx 3 S	3	6	2600	100	32
dryfit 3 Fx 5 S	3	6	7500	500	31
dryfit 6 Fx 3 S	6	12	4500	500	14
Special batteries 1 Ks 5	1	2	6000	500	19
Various types					
6 N 4	3	6	4000	500	16
Matsushita	3	6	4000	500-1000	30-10
Yuasa	3	6	11000	550-1100	30-15

Table 2 Scales and their Square Roots

scale	√	scale	√	scale	√
1:20	4,75	1:40	6,3	1:75	8,7
1:25	5	1:45	6,7	1:80	8,9
1:30	5,5	1:50	7,1	1:90	9,5
1:35	5,9	1:60	7,7	1:100	10

Table 3 Tangents of Angles between 10° and 49°

°	tan	°	tan	°	tan	°	tan
10	0,18	**20**	0,36	**30**	0,58	**40**	0,84
11	0,19	21	0,38	31	0,60	41	0,87
12	0,21	22	0,40	32	0,62	42	0,90
13	0,23	23	0,42	33	0,65	43	0,93
14	0,25	24	0,45	34	0,67	44	0,97
15	0,27	25	0,47	35	0,70	45	1
16	0,29	26	0,49	36	0,73	46	1,04
17	0,31	27	0,51	37	0,75	47	1,07
18	0,32	28	0,53	38	0,78	48	1,11
19	0,34	29	0,55	39	0,81	49	1,15

Basic Switching Systems for Electric Motor Drives

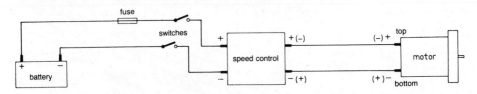

A. Switching with speed control. As drawn, the motor is set to go ahead, but the speed controller can reverse the polarity (shown in brackets) to make it go astern. The whole range of speeds from full ahead to full astern is steplessly variable.

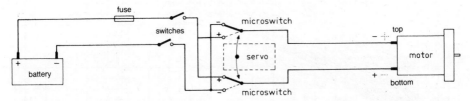

B. Switching without speed control. Here two double switches and a servo are used to reverse the polarity (shown dotted) when required.

Fig I Optimum Conditions

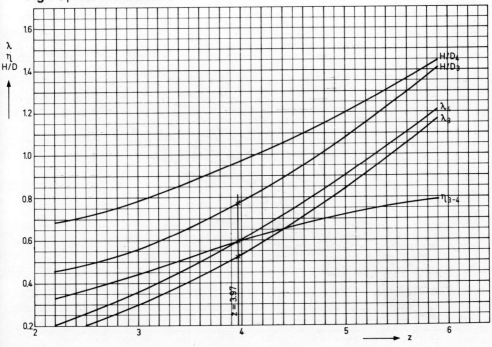

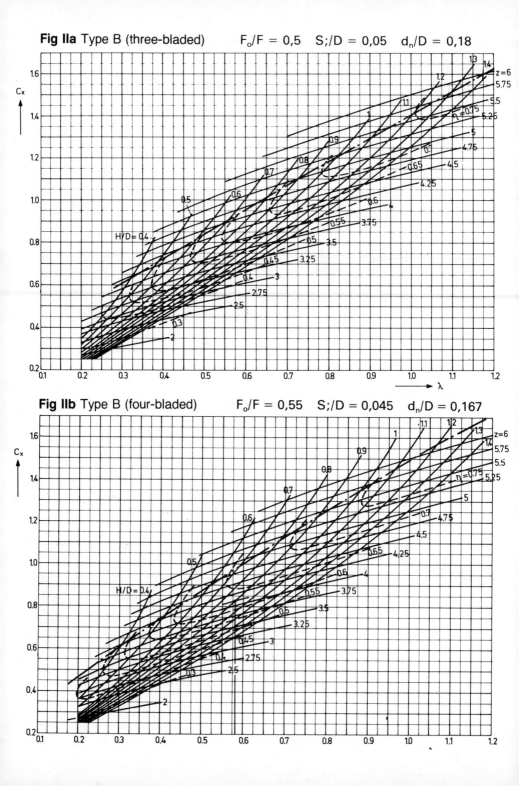

Fig IIa Type B (three-bladed) $F_o/F = 0,5$ $S_i/D = 0,05$ $d_n/D = 0,18$

Fig IIb Type B (four-bladed) $F_o/F = 0,55$ $S_i/D = 0,045$ $d_n/D = 0,167$

Fig IIIa Monoperm (TM, 6 V)

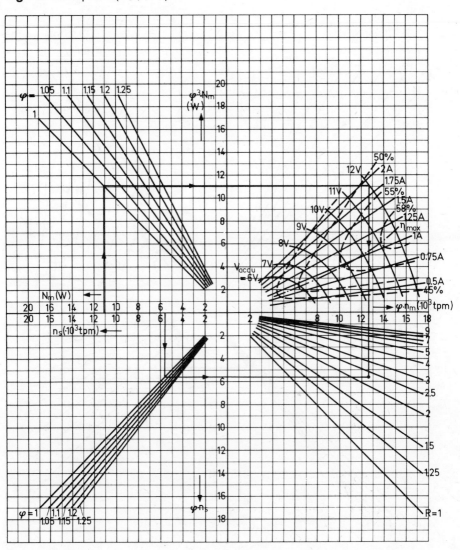

$$V_{brush} = V_{battery} - 1$$

Fig IIIb Monoperm super (TMS, 6 V)

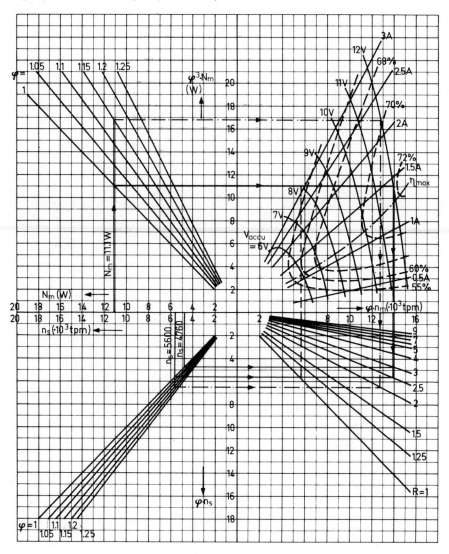

$$V_{brush} = V_{battery} - 1$$

Fig IIIb (TMS, 6 V) without reduction

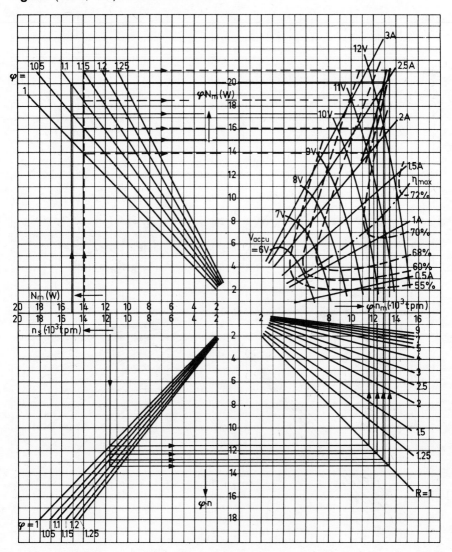

$$V_{brush} = V_{battery} - 1$$

Fig IIIc Decaperm (TD, 6 V)

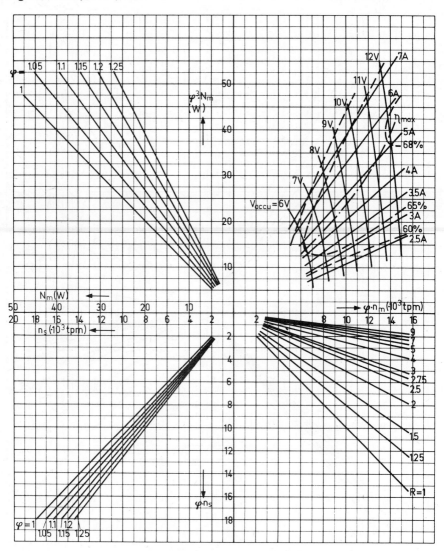

$$V_{brush} = V_{battery} - 1$$

Fig IIId Hectoperm (TH, 6 V)

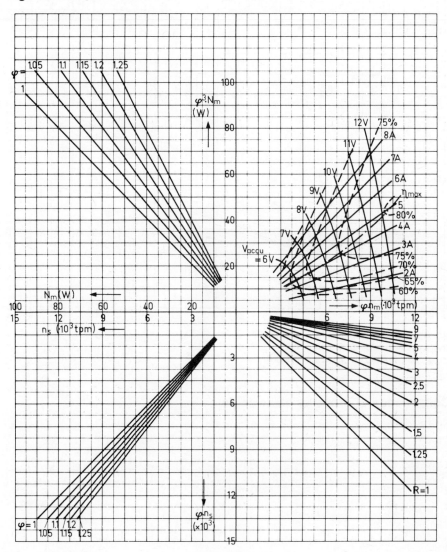

$V_{brush} = V_{battery} - 1$

Fig IV Graupner propellers

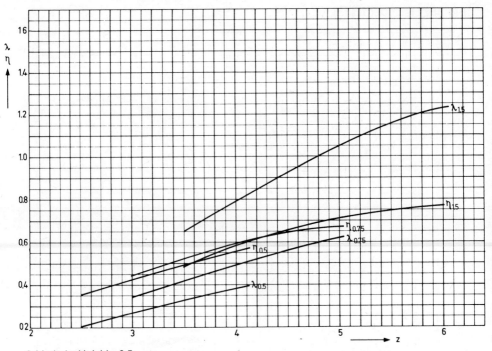

3-bladed with h/d =0,5
2-bladed with h/d =0,75 (speed)
2-bladed with h/d =1,5 (double-speed)

Construction of propeller blade angle

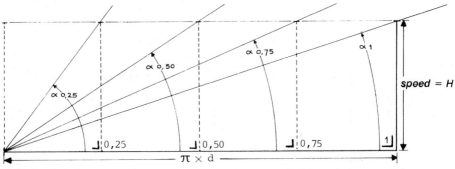

propeller dia = d   propeller circumference = π × d

angle   0.25 = blade angle on 25% of max propeller diameter
angle   0.50 = blade angle on 50% of max propeller diameter
angle   0.75 = blade angle on 75% of max propeller diameter
angle   1.00 = blade angle on max propeller diameter

APPENDIX 3 Electric Motors

motor	voltage V	length mm	width mm	height mm	shaft dia mm	weight g	speed rpm	transmission
Orbit 005	1,5- 3	25,4	20,6	20,6	2	18	10000	
Orbit 105	1,5- 3	28,6	20,6	20,6	2	25	9000	
Orbit 205	1,5- 3	28,6	25,4	25,4	2	32	9000	
Orbit 305	1,5- 3	31,8	25,4	25,4	2,3	39	6500	
Orbit 405	1,5- 6	31,8	31,8	31,8	2,3	53	10500	
Orbit 505	1,5- 6	34,9	31,8	31,8	2,3	67	9000	
Orbit 605	4,5- 6	50,8	34,9	34,9	3,2	92	9000	
Orbit 705	4 - 8	50,8	34,9	34,9	3,2	142	7000	
Orbit 805	6 -12	60,3	44,5	44,5	4	262	9000	
Atom	1,5- 3	31,8	20,6	15,9	2	28	11000	
Micromax T 03	2 - 4	19	19	19	2	25	330	60:1
Micromax T 03	2 - 4	19	19	19	2	25	1200	15:1
Micromax T 05	2	15,9	15,9	15,9	t.w.	14	18000	
Micromax T 05	2	17,5	15,9	15,9	2	4	410	41:1
Micromax T 05	2	17,5	15,9	15,9	2	5	128	141:1
Micromax T 05	2	19	15,9	15,9	2	7	37	485:1
Jumbo 2000	6	63,1	34,9	34,9	2	142	8000	
Jumbo 2000 F	12	88,5	34,9	34,9	4	184	2000	5:1
Monoperm Super	6	46	30	30	2	90	6000	3, 6, 12, 16, 32 or 60:1
Richard I	6	87	40	47	4	57	8000	3, 6, 12, 16, 32 or 60:1
Richard II	6	97	40	47	4	153	6000	3, 6, 12, 16, 32 or 60:1
Mini Richard	6	37	37	25	2	18	6000	3, 6, 12, 32 or 60:1
Microperm Spl.	2 - 6	26	17	21	1,5	16	13000	
Milliperm Spl.	6	34	21	28	1,5	26	10000	
Monoperm Spl.	6	40	30	30	2	75	11000	
Monoperm S/Spl.	6	52	30	30	2	120	8000	
Decaperm Spl.	6	62	44	55	4	370	3000	2,75:1
Hectoperm Spl.	6	65	52	52	4	600	6000	2:1
Milliperm S/Pile	6	70	24	24	3	70	10000	3:1 to 360:1
Monoperm S/Pile	6	121	36	50	4	95	11000	3:1 to 360:1
Decaperm S/Pile	6	169,5	52	52	6	420	9000	3:1 to 360:1
Hectoperm S/Pile	6	181,5	52	52	6	710	6000	3:1 to 360:1
Target	6 -12	38,1	41,3	66,7	2,4	228	6000	
Meteor	6 -12	44,5	41,3	66,7	2,4	341	6500	
Standard	6 -12	76,2	41,3	66,7	4,8	512	10000	
Supermarine	6 -12	76,2	104,4	57,2	6,4	909	4500	
D/Supermarine Spl.	6 -12	76,2	104,4	57,2	6,4	1134	10000	